Witchcraft as Healing

Harnessing the Power of Witchcraft for Inner Well-being

Katherine Mitchell

© Copyright 2023 - All rights reserved.

The content contained within this book may not be reproduced, duplicated or transmitted without direct written permission from the author or the publisher.

Under no circumstances will any blame or legal responsibility be held against the publisher, or author, for any damages, reparation, or monetary loss due to the information contained within this book, either directly or indirectly.

Legal Notice:

This book is copyright protected. It is only for personal use. You cannot amend, distribute, sell, use, quote or paraphrase any part, or the content within this book, without the consent of the author or publisher.

Disclaimer Notice:

Please note the information contained within this document is for educational and entertainment purposes only. All effort has been executed to present accurate, up to date, reliable, complete information. No warranties of any kind are declared or implied. Readers acknowledge that the author is not engaging in the rendering of legal, financial, medical or professional advice. The content within this book has been derived from various sources. Please consult a licensed professional before attempting any techniques outlined in this book.

By reading this document, the reader agrees that under no circumstances is the author responsible for any losses, direct or indirect, that are incurred as a result of the use of information contained within this document, including, but not limited to, errors, omissions, or inaccuracies.

Table of Contents

INTRODUCTION 5
   Definition of witchcraft therapy 5
   Brief history of witchcraft as a therapeutic tool 8
   The benefits of using witchcraft as a therapeutic tool . 11
   How this book will aid readers grow through witchcraft
   13

CHAPTER I: Understanding Witchcraft as a Therapeutic Tool 16
   The concept of energy in witchcraft therapy 16
   Using witchcraft for self-reflection and introspection .. 18
   How witchcraft can help with emotional healing 20
   How witchcraft can help with physical healing 22

CHAPTER II: Getting Started with Witchcraft Therapy 24
   Creating a sacred space for witchcraft therapy 24
   Choosing and consecrating tools for witchcraft therapy
   29
   Preparing yourself for witchcraft therapy 36
   The importance of intention setting in witchcraft therapy 58

CHAPTER III: Techniques and Practices for Witchcraft Therapy 63
   Meditation and visualization 63

Spellwork and ritual 73

Divination and tarot reading 83

Herbalism and aromatherapy 94

CHAPTER IV: Applying Witchcraft Therapy for Personal Growth 102

Overcoming negative patterns and behaviors 102

Developing self-awareness and self-acceptance 107

Strengthening intuition and spiritual connection 112

Creating a sense of empowerment and self-worth 117

CHAPTER V: Incorporating Witchcraft Therapy into Your Daily Life 123

Developing a daily witchcraft practice 123

Maintaining a connection to nature and the seasons 128

Finding a community of like-minded individuals 132

Integrating witchcraft into your spiritual practice 137

CONCLUSION 141

Summary of witchcraft's therapeutic benefits 141

Final ideas and encouragement to use witchcraft for self-improvement 143

INTRODUCTION

Definition of witchcraft therapy

Witchcraft therapy is a sort of alternative treatment that blends aspects of witchcraft and psychotherapy to encourage spiritual development, emotional healing, and personal growth. This type of therapy is also known as "magickal therapy" or "witchy therapy," and it is gaining popularity among individuals seeking a holistic approach to mental health and well-being.

Witchcraft therapy is based on the fundamental principles of witchcraft, which include the conviction that all things are interrelated and that energy may be controlled and manipulated by means of ritual and purpose. Psychology-related ideas like the significance of self-reflection, self-awareness, and the need to heal emotional traumas are also incorporated into witchcraft therapy.

Witchcraft therapy is not just for people who practice paganism or witchcraft. Anyone who is interested in employing alternative techniques for healing and personal development is welcome. Additionally, it's important to understand that for people with severe mental illnesses, witchcraft therapy shouldn't take the place of conventional therapies or medications. Instead, it can be used as an addition to conventional therapy.

The idea of energy is one of the key concepts in witchcraft therapy. In witchcraft, energy is seen as the force that connects all things in the universe. Through ceremony and intention, this energy can be captured and focused. In witchcraft therapy, patients are urged to become conscious of their energy and learn how to harness it for the accomplishment of their desires and goals.

The application of symbolism and metaphor is an important concept in witchcraft therapy. The pentacle, the moon, and the elements of earth, air, fire, and water are just a few of the many symbols used in witchcraft. These symbols can be utilized in therapy as a means of representing feelings, ideas, and experiences. Fire, for instance, might stand in for rage or passion, whereas water can stand in for emotions and the subconscious mind.

Individuals are also urged to make a connection with nature throughout witchcraft therapy. Nature has been regarded as a place of solace and enlightenment. Spending time in nature, meditating outside, and practicing rituals that honor the natural world can be a powerful tool for personal growth and healing.

Witchcraft therapy uses a number of approaches that can be customized to meet the unique requirements and objectives of each patient. The use of ritual, spellwork, divination, visualization, meditation, and herbalism are some of the methods employed in witchcraft therapy.

Meditation is a key component of witchcraft therapy. It is a technique that helps individuals in being more conscious of their thoughts, feelings, and bodily sensations. The mind can be calmed, stress and anxiety can be reduced, and attention and clarity can be improved by meditation.

Visualization is another technique used in witchcraft therapy. It involves using one's imagination to produce mental images that serve as representations of objectives, intentions, or desired results. The use of visualization can boost inspiration, soothe anxiety, and encourage optimistic thinking.

Ritual is a technique for achieving a specific goal or impact by using symbols and intention. Rituals can be as simple as lighting a candle or as complex as a full moon ceremony. Rituals can be utilized to signal changes, let go of bad energy, and encourage healing and transformation.

Spellwork is another technique used in witchcraft therapy. Spells are a type of intention-setting that entails the use of words, symbols, and physical things to produce a particular result. Spells can be employed for a variety of purposes, such as luring good fortune and love, driving away evil, and fostering healing.

Tarot cards, runes, or pendulums are a few examples of the tools used in the practice of divination, which aims to provide insight into the past, present, or future. Clarity, decision-making, and the exploration of feelings and thoughts can all be achieved through divination.

The practice of herbalism involves using plants and herbs for health and healing. Herbs can be used to enhance the immune system or relieve pain, for example, in order to promote physical health. It can also be used for emotional and spiritual healing, such as using herbs for relaxation or to promote a sense of grounding and balance.

The purpose of witchcraft therapy is to establish a sacred and safe environment for one's own development and healing. The establishment of a personal altar or sacred place, the use of certain tools or objects, and the creation of rituals and practices that foster a sense of connection and intention can all help with this.

It is essential to understand that witchcraft therapy does not serve as a substitute for conventional therapies or medications. Instead, it is a complimentary strategy that may be applied along with other types of therapy to encourage holistic healing and wellness.

In summary up, witchcraft therapy is a type of complementary treatment that blends aspects of witchcraft and psychotherapy in order to encourage spiritual development, emotional healing, and personal progress.. It is based on the principles of witchcraft, which include the belief that everything in the universe is interconnected and that energy can be directed and manipulated through intention and ritual. Witchcraft treatment uses a range of techniques and practices, such as visualization, ritual, spellwork, divination, meditation, and herbalism, to assist clients in realizing their intentions and goals. Witchcraft treatment can be a potent tool for those looking for a holistic approach to mental health and well-being, even though it shouldn't replace conventional therapies or medications.

Brief history of witchcraft as a therapeutic tool

The history of using witchcraft as a therapeutic technique is long and complex, dating back many centuries. The use of witchcraft for healing and spiritual growth dates back to ancient times, despite the fact that modern witchcraft therapy has its roots in the 20th century.

The use of magic and healing was closely associated with spirituality and religion in many ancient cultures. For instance, priests and priestesses in ancient Egypt used spells and incantations to heal the sick and ward off evil spirits. In ancient Greece, women known as pharmakides used herbs and potions to heal the body and the mind.

In the Middle Ages, witchcraft acquired a bad reputation, and women who were charged with using black magic to harm others were referred to as "witches." However, a lot of these women were also healers, midwives, and herbalists who benefited their communities by using what they learned about plants and herbal treatments.

Interest in witchcraft and magic started to resurface in the late 19th and early 20th centuries. The rise of spiritualism and occultism, as well as the influence of individuals like Aleister Crowley and Helena Blavatsky, were some of the causes of this. The idea of modern witchcraft, or Wicca, started to take shape at this time. Gerald Gardner, a British civil servant who founded modern witchcraft, developed an interest in the occult in the 1930s. Gardner claimed to have been initiated into a coven of witches who practiced an ancient religion based on the worship of a horned god and a mother goddess. He published a number of works on the subject, such as "Witchcraft Today" and "The Meaning of Witchcraft," which contributed to the spread of the idea of modern witchcraft.

The feminist movement and the counterculture revolution both contributed to the increased acceptance of witchcraft and other alternative spiritual practices in the 1960s and 1970s. In order to reclaim their independence and power as well as to identify with a spiritual tradition that honored the feminine, many women turned to witchcraft.

At this time, the idea of using witchcraft as a therapeutic tool started to take hold. Witchcraft and rituals became popular tools used by practitioners to aid in healing and personal development. The emphasis was on using witchcraft as a means of self-reflection emotional healing, and spiritual growth.

In the 1980s and 90s, the concept of "magickal therapy" began to gain popularity. This method of therapy combined elements of psychotherapy and witchcraft. Practitioners assisted patients in achieving their therapeutic objectives using a range of methods, such as ritual, spellwork, visualization, and meditation.

Witchcraft therapy is a developing field today that uses a range of methods and strategies. While some practitioners concentrate on traditional witchcraft, others incorporate elements of Buddhism or shamanism into their practices. The emphasis is on utilizing witchcraft as a tool for spiritual development, emotional healing, and personal growth.

The idea of intention is one of the fundamental ideas in witchcraft therapy. In witchcraft, intention is a potent force that can be employed to realize goals and effect transformation. In therapy, intention is used to concentrate on particular outcomes and goals. Practitioners work with clients to determine their intentions and assist them create rituals and techniques to help them reach their objectives.

The use of symbolism and metaphor is another important concept in witchcraft therapy. Practitioners use symbols, such as the elements, tarot cards, or crystals, to represent emotions, thoughts, and experiences. These symbols can be used in therapy as a way to explore and process feelings, and to promote healing and transformation.

In addition to these techniques, many practitioners of witchcraft therapy incorporate practices such as journaling, dream work, and working with spirit guides or ancestors. Journaling can be used to track progress and reflect on experiences, while dream work can be used to explore the subconscious mind and gain insight into deeper emotions and desires. Working with spirit guides or ancestors can provide guidance and support on the spiritual path.

While witchcraft therapy is often associated with alternative forms of spirituality, it is important to note that it is not limited to individuals who practice witchcraft or paganism. Witchcraft therapy is open to anyone who is interested in using alternative methods for personal growth and healing. It's also crucial to remember that for individuals with severe mental illnesses, witchcraft therapy shouldn't take the place of conventional therapies or prescription drugs.

Overall, the brief history of witchcraft as a healing practice reflects the enduring need for connection, meaning, and healing in human beings. People have used magic, religion, and spirituality throughout history to get through difficult times and to connect with something greater than themselves. Witchcraft therapy, which emphasizes the interconnectedness of mind, body, and spirit, carries on this tradition by offering people a holistic approach to mental health and well-being.

The benefits of using witchcraft as a therapeutic tool

Witchcraft as a therapeutic tool has a wide range of advantages. Witchcraft therapy emphasizes the connection between the mind, body, and spirit as part of a holistic approach to mental health and wellbeing. By incorporating elements of witchcraft and psychotherapy, individuals can gain a deeper understanding of themselves, develop new coping skills, and promote personal growth and transformation.

The focus on self-awareness and self-reflection that comes with using witchcraft as a therapeutic tool is one of its main advantages. Witchcraft teaches people how to use their increased awareness of their thoughts, feelings, and bodily sensations as a tool for healing and personal development. People can gain insight into their emotions and behavior and find new ways to cope with stress and anxiety by learning to be more mindful and reflective.

Witchcraft therapy also promotes healing and transformation through the use of ritual and symbolism. A sense of connection and intention can be fostered through rituals, which can also be used to mark transitions and release negative energy. Symbols, such as tarot cards or crystals, can be used to represent emotions, thoughts, and experiences, and can be used in therapy as a way to explore and process feelings. Witchcraft therapy also emphasizes the importance of intention setting. In witchcraft, intention is a potent force that can be employed to realize goals and effect change. In therapy, intention is used to concentrate on particular outcomes and goals. Practitioners work with clients to determine their intentions and help them create rituals and techniques to help them reach their objectives.

The emphasis on spirituality and a connection to nature is another advantage of using witchcraft as a therapeutic tool. Witchcraft teaches people to communicate with the natural world, including the earth, the seasons, and its cycles. This connection can give one a sense of stability and equilibrium and can encourage a more profound sense of meaning and purpose.

Witchcraft therapy has a number of additional advantages, including the ability to treat a range of mental health issues. For example, meditation and visualization can be used to reduce stress and anxiety, while spellwork can be used to promote positive thinking and self-esteem. Divination and tarot reading can be used to gain insight into past traumas or negative patterns, and to explore feelings of grief, loss, or anxiety.

Witchcraft therapy can also be used to promote physical health and well-being. Herbalism, for example, can be used to support the immune system or to relieve pain and inflammation. Aromatherapy can be used to promote relaxation and reduce stress, while meditation and visualization can be used to reduce blood pressure and promote overall health.

Overall, the benefits of using witchcraft as a therapeutic tool reflect the growing interest in alternative forms of therapy and the recognition of the interconnectedness of mind, body, and spirit. By incorporating elements of witchcraft and psychotherapy, individuals can gain a deeper understanding of themselves and their emotions, develop new coping skills, and promote personal growth and transformation. Whether used as a complementary approach to traditional therapy or as a standalone practice, witchcraft therapy has the potential to promote holistic healing and well-being for individuals seeking a deeper connection to themselves and the world around them.

How this book will aid readers grow through witchcraft

The purpose of the book "Witchcraft as Healing: Harnessing the Power of Witchcraft for Inner Well-being" is to teach readers how to use witchcraft as a tool for spiritual development, emotional healing, and personal growth. This book offers a holistic strategy for mental health and wellbeing that emphasizes the connection between mind, body, and spirit by combining aspects of witchcraft and psychotherapy.

In order to help readers understand how to use witchcraft for personal growth, the book is divided into a number of sections. Witchcraft therapy is introduced in the first section, along with a definition of the term and a synopsis of how it took place . This section also outlines the benefits of using witchcraft as a therapeutic tool and how the book will help readers achieve their goals.

The second part of the book explains how witchcraft can be used as a therapeutic tool. This section examines the idea of energy in witchcraft therapy and shows how it can be used for healing and personal development. It also looks at the use of witchcraft in self-reflection and introspection, emotional healing, and physical healing.

The third chapter of the book is intended to help readers in beginning witchcraft therapy. This section discusses the value of setting up a sacred environment for witchcraft therapy, selecting and consecrating tools, and getting ready for the practice. Additionally, it discusses the significance of intention setting in witchcraft therapy and offers advice on how to do it successfully.

The techniques and practices for witchcraft therapy are the subject of the fourth chapter of the book. This section explores several different techniques that can be used to promote personal growth and healing, including meditation and visualization, spellwork and ritual, divination and tarot reading, and herbalism and aromatherapy. Each approach is well explained, and readers are given instructions on how to apply it to their own practice.

The book's fifth section is intended to teach readers how to use witchcraft treatment for personal development. This section looks at how witchcraft therapy can help people break bad habits and behaviors, become more self-aware and accepting of who they are, enhance their spiritual connection and intuition, and feel more empowered and self-worth. It also offers advice on how to discover a group of like-minded people, establish a daily witchcraft practice, stay connected to nature and the seasons, and incorporate witchcraft into one's spiritual practice.

The book's conclusion summarizes the advantages of utilizing witchcraft as a therapeutic technique and encourages readers to keep practicing witchcraft for their own personal development and healing. It also provides resources for further learning and exploration, including books, websites, and online communities.

The overall goal of this book is to teach readers how to utilize witchcraft as a tool for healing and personal development. It discusses the many techniques and practices that can be employed to encourage healing and personal growth while giving a thorough introduction of witchcraft therapy. This book offers a holistic strategy for mental health and wellbeing that anybody can adopt, regardless of their spiritual or religious views by combining parts of witchcraft and psychotherapy. Whether utilized as an independent practice or as a complimentary approach to standard treatment, this book has the potential to help readers achieve deeper self-awareness, emotional healing, and spiritual connection.

CHAPTER I

Understanding Witchcraft as a Therapeutic Tool

The concept of energy in witchcraft therapy

Witchcraft therapy places a strong emphasis on the idea of energy. In witchcraft, energy is viewed as a universal force that permeates all things and can be harnessed and directed to promote personal growth and healing. Practitioners of witchcraft therapy employ a range of methods and practices to deal with energy and promote their patients' emotional, physical, and spiritual well-being.

The idea that everything in the universe is interconnected is one of the fundamental ideas of energy in witchcraft therapy. People, animals, plants, minerals, and even inanimate objects are included in this. According to this viewpoint, everything is made of energy and communicates with one other continually. Changes in one component of the system can have an impact on all other components due to its interconnection.

The significance of harmony and balance in the movement of energy is also emphasized in witchcraft therapy. Energy that is balanced and free to flow promotes health and vitality. Physical, emotional, or spiritual sickness can result from obstructed or stagnant energy. Witchcraft therapy teaches individuals how to work with their own energy and the energy of the universe to promote balance and flow.

Meditation and visualization are two of the main methods employed in witchcraft therapy to work with energy. During meditation, practitioners focus their attention on their breath or a specific visualization, such as a calming image or a specific color. This concentration aids in mind peace, relaxation, and an openness to the flow of energy.

Visualization is also used to direct and manipulate energy. Practitioners visualize the movement of energy through their own bodies or a particular body part, such the throat or the heart. They may also see energy entering or leaving a particular thing or person. By releasing any blockages or energy that has become stagnant, this visualization helps in promoting the flow of energy.

Spellwork and ritual are another two important methods utilized in witchcraft therapy to work with energy. Spells and rituals are designed to direct and manipulate energy to achieve a specific outcome. Spells may involve the use of candles, crystals, or herbs, and may be designed to promote healing, protection, or abundance. Rituals may involve the use of specific movements or gestures, the recitation of specific words or incantations, or the use of specific objects or tools.

Divination and tarot reading are also used in witchcraft therapy to work with energy. Divination tools, such as tarot cards or runes, are used to gain insight into past traumas or negative patterns, and to explore feelings of grief, loss, or anxiety. These tools can also be used to identify areas of blocked or stagnant energy and to develop strategies for releasing that energy and promoting balance and flow.

Herbalism and aromatherapy are also used in witchcraft therapy to work with energy. Certain herbs and essential oils are believed to have specific energetic properties, such as promoting relaxation, reducing stress, or promoting physical healing. These herbs and oils can be used in teas, tinctures, or inhaled as part of a meditation or visualization practice.

Overall, the concept of energy in witchcraft therapy reflects the idea that everything is composed of energy and is constantly interacting with everything else. By working with their own energy and the energy of the universe, individuals can promote balance and flow, and achieve greater emotional, physical, and spiritual well-being. Through meditation, visualization, spellwork, and other techniques, practitioners of witchcraft therapy can gain a deeper understanding of the energetic nature of the universe and harness that energy to promote personal growth and healing.

Using witchcraft for self-reflection and introspection

Using witchcraft for self-reflection and introspection is an important aspect of witchcraft therapy. Self-reflection and introspection involve examining one's thoughts, emotions, and behaviors in order to gain insight and awareness. In witchcraft therapy, practitioners use a variety of techniques and practices to promote self- reflection and introspection, including meditation, journaling, divination, and ritual.

Meditation is a powerful tool for self-reflection and introspection. During meditation, practitioners focus their attention on their breath or a specific visualization, such as a calming image or a specific color. This focus helps to quiet the mind and promote a state of relaxation and openness to self-exploration. Practitioners may use guided meditations specifically designed for self- reflection, such as ones that focus on exploring one's inner landscape or connecting with a particular archetype.

Journaling is another effective tool for self-reflection and introspection. By putting one's thoughts and feelings onto paper, practitioners are able to gain clarity and insight into their inner landscape. Journaling can also be used to track progress, identify patterns, and explore emotions that may be difficult to express verbally.

Divination is a powerful tool for gaining insight into oneself. Divination tools, such as tarot cards or runes, can be used to gain insight into past traumas or negative patterns, and to explore feelings of grief, loss, or anxiety. These tools can also be used to identify areas of blocked or stagnant energy and to develop strategies for releasing that energy and promoting balance and flow.

Rituals can also be used for self-reflection and introspection. Practitioners can design rituals specifically for self-exploration, such as ones that focus on releasing negative patterns or connecting with one's inner child. The use of symbols and metaphors during rituals can help practitioners gain a deeper understanding of their emotions and behaviors and identify areas that may need further exploration.

Another important aspect of using witchcraft for self-reflection and introspection is the focus on personal responsibility. Witchcraft emphasizes the idea that individuals are responsible for their own thoughts, emotions, and behaviors. By taking responsibility for one's own actions and reactions, practitioners are able to gain a deeper understanding of themselves and develop new coping strategies.

In general, employing witchcraft for introspection and self-reflection highlights the significance of developing consciousness and insight into one's inner world. Practitioners of witchcraft treatment can better understand their thoughts, feelings, and actions by utilizing a range of techniques and practices. They can also create new coping mechanisms and interpersonal relationships. Practitioners can foster self-awareness and self-acceptance as well as personal growth and healing through ritual, divination, journaling, and meditation.

How witchcraft can help with emotional healing

Witchcraft therapy can be a powerful tool for emotional healing. Witchcraft therapy promotes holistic healing and well-being by combining traditional psychotherapy with spirituality and alternative healing modalities. By working with energy, symbols, ritual, and intention, practitioners of witchcraft therapy can help individuals heal from emotional trauma and develop new coping skills.

One of the key ways that witchcraft can help with emotional healing is by providing a safe and supportive environment for individuals to explore and express their emotions. Witchcraft emphasizes the value of creating a sacred space for treatment where people feel comfortable sharing their thoughts and feelings without fear of judgment. For those who have undergone trauma or are dealing with powerful emotions, this might be especially important.

In witchcraft therapy, visualization and meditation are also effective techniques for emotional rehabilitation. A stronger sense of inner peace and calmness can be attained through meditation, and the practice of mindfulness can improve one's capacity to control their emotions. Visualization is a tool that people can use to explore their emotions in a safe and controlled way. It can also help people in letting go of negative emotions and cultivating more optimistic self-talk and coping mechanisms.

In witchcraft treatment, rituals can also help individuals heal emotionally. Rituals can be used to mark important life events, such as transitions or grief, and can help individuals release negative emotions and promote positive emotions, such as gratitude or self-love. Practitioners can also design rituals specifically for emotional healing, such as ones that focus on releasing negative patterns or connecting with one's inner child. Divination and tarot reading can also be used to promote emotional healing in witchcraft therapy. These tools can be used to gain insight into past traumas or negative patterns, and to explore feelings of grief, loss, or anxiety. Practitioners can work with clients to identify patterns and triggers and develop strategies for coping with difficult emotions.

Spellwork can also be used to promote emotional healing in witchcraft therapy. Spells can be designed to promote emotional healing and release negative emotions, such as spells for self-love or protection. Practitioners can work with clients to identify their intentions and develop spells that are tailored to their specific needs.

Herbalism and aromatherapy are also powerful tools for emotional healing in witchcraft therapy. Certain herbs and essential oils are believed to have specific emotional properties, such as promoting relaxation, reducing stress, or promoting emotional healing. Practitioners can work with clients to identify the herbs and oils that are best suited for their emotional needs and develop personalized remedies, such as teas or oils.

Overall, witchcraft therapy can be a powerful tool for emotional healing. By working with energy, symbols, ritual, and intention, practitioners of witchcraft therapy can help individuals heal from emotional trauma and develop new coping skills. Through meditation, visualization, rituals, divination, spellwork, and herbalism, practitioners can promote emotional healing and well-being for individuals seeking a deeper connection to themselves and the world around them.

How witchcraft can help with physical healing

Witchcraft can be a powerful tool for physical healing. Witchcraft therapy combines elements of traditional medicine, energy work, and spiritual practices to promote holistic healing and well-being. By working with energy, herbs, and intention, practitioners of witchcraft therapy can help individuals heal from physical ailments and promote a greater sense of physical well-being.

By encouraging relaxation and stress reduction, witchcraft can help in physical healing in a number of important ways. Witchcraft treatment can help in reducing stress and promoting physical healing because stress can have a negative effect on one's physical health. Particularly helpful techniques for encouraging relaxation and lowering stress include visualization and meditation. Practitioners can collaborate with patients to determine the bodily regions affected by stress and create individualized visualization or meditation routines to encourage healing and relaxation.

Another effective method of physical healing used in witchcraft therapy is herbalism. It is thought that certain herbs have particular healing characteristics and can be utilized to encourage physical healing. For example, chamomile is often used for relaxation and sleep, while ginger is used for digestion and inflammation. Practitioners can work with clients to identify the specific herbs that are best suited for their physical needs and develop personalized remedies, such as teas or tinctures.

Aromatherapy is also a powerful tool for physical healing in witchcraft therapy. Essential oils are believed to have specific healing properties and can be used to promote physical healing. For example, lavender is often used for relaxation and sleep, while eucalyptus is used for respiratory issues. Practitioners can work with clients to identify the specific essential oils that are best suited for their physical needs and develop personalized remedies, such as massage oils or inhalers.

Energy work is another key aspect of physical healing in witchcraft therapy. Practitioners can work with clients to identify areas of blocked or stagnant energy and use energy work techniques, such as Reiki, to promote the flow of energy and promote physical healing. Energy work can also be used to promote relaxation and reduce stress, which can have a positive impact on physical health.

Spellwork and ritual can also be used to promote physical healing in witchcraft therapy. Spells and rituals can be designed to promote physical healing, such as spells for pain relief or rituals for body positivity. Practitioners can work with clients to identify their intentions and develop spells and rituals that are tailored to their specific needs. Overall, witchcraft therapy can be a powerful tool for physical healing. By working with energy, herbs, and intention, practitioners of witchcraft therapy can help individuals heal from physical ailments and promote a greater sense of physical well-being. Through meditation, visualization, herbalism, aromatherapy, energy work, spellwork, and ritual, practitioners can promote physical healing and well-being for individuals seeking a deeper connection to themselves and the world around them.

CHAPTER II

Getting Started with Witchcraft Therapy

Creating a sacred space for witchcraft therapy

A key component of witchcraft therapy that contributes to the establishment of an environment of security, connection, and empowerment is the creation of a sacred place. A physical or emotional area that has been set aside particularly for healing, personal development, and self-discovery is called a sacred space. Witchcraft therapy practitioners can assist patients in feeling supported, validated, and understood during treatment sessions by helping to create a sacred space.

Setting an intention and building an environment that reflects it both physically and emotionally constitute the establishment of a sacred space. Setting an intention is essential to creating a sacred space since it determines the space's main function and energy. The aim may be specific to the client's session or it may be broad and apply to all therapy sessions. The intention of the sacred space might be to create a nurturing environment that facilitates healing, to promote spiritual connection and exploration, or to foster a sense of safety and empowerment.

The physical area is another key part of creating a sacred space. The physical area should be uncluttered, free of distractions, and created in a way that encourages comfort and relaxation. To create a peaceful and relaxing environment, practitioners should offer comfortable chairs, delicate lighting, and calming music. In order to improve the energy of the place, practitioners may also add personal symbols and items like crystals, candles, or spiritual objects.

Another crucial element in creating a sacred space is the emotional space. This refers to the space's energy and emotional atmosphere, which is just as important as the actual physical space. Practitioners should be present, attentive, and non-judgmental throughout therapy sessions, offering validation, empathy, and support to individuals. Through active listening and validation, practitioners can foster a sense of connection and trust with the individual, which is essential for creating a safe and supportive emotional space.

A sacred place can be made for witchcraft therapy using effective tools like meditation and visualization.

Individuals can connect with their inner selves and acquire a sense of peace and serenity with the help of practitioners who can lead them through visualization or meditation activities that encourage relaxation and calm. Individuals can visualize the sacred space in their minds by engaging in visualization exercises, which enables them to picture themselves in a serene and encouraging setting.

Rituals and spells can also be utilized to create a sacred place for witchcraft therapy. These techniques can empower individuals spiritually and foster a sense of spiritual connection by assisting individuals in connecting with the space's intention. Practitioners can design rituals or spells that involve lighting candles or incense, using specific objects or symbols, or performing specific actions that promote a sense of connection and groundingThese techniques can be personalized for each person and help in healing, development, and self-discovery.

The advantages of setting up a sacred space for witchcraft therapy are numerous. Individuals can feel more relaxed and at ease in a sacred space, which encourages greater openness and in-depth exploration of feelings and experiences. By enabling people to connect with their inner selves and access their natural healing skills, the sacred space can also assist to foster a sense of spiritual empowerment. The sacred space can also promote a sense of community and support, fostering an environment where individuals feel heard, understood, and validated.

Witchcraft therapy practitioners can create a sacred space that meets their needs and preferences by utilizing a range of strategies and rituals. Here are some additional methods that can be used to create a sacred space for witchcraft therapy:

Smudging

Smudging is a ritual practice that involves burning sage, palo santo, or other herbs to cleanse the energy of a space. This practice is often used at the beginning of a therapy session to clear any negative energy and set the intention for the sacred space. Smudging can be a powerful tool for creating a sense of calm and purification in the space, and it can also promote spiritual connection and grounding.

Altars

An altar is a space that is set aside for spiritual or ritual purposes, and it can be a powerful tool for creating a sacred space for witchcraft therapy. Altars can be simple or elaborate, and they can include objects such as candles, crystals, statues, or other spiritual objects. Practitioners can work with individuals to create an altar that reflects their intention for the sacred space and includes objects that are meaningful to them.

Sound Healing

Utilizing sound, such as that produced by singing bowls, gongs, or chimes, to encourage healing and relaxation is known as sound healing. In order to promote relaxation and a stronger sense of connection to oneself and the world around us, practitioners can utilize sound healing techniques to instill a sense of serenity and harmony in the sacred space.

Guided Imagery

Guided imagery is a practice that uses visualization to promote healing and relaxation. A visualization practice that enables people to connect with their inner selves and utilize their underlying healing skills can be led by practitioners. In the sacred space, guided imagery can be a powerful tool for encouraging calm and relaxation, enabling people to more fully examine their feelings and experiences.

Sacred Objects

Sacred objects can be added by practitioners to the sacred space to foster a sense of connection and grounding. Sacred objects can include crystals, talismans, or other objects that have personal or spiritual significance. These objects can be used to promote a sense of calm and connection in the space, allowing individuals to feel more comfortable and at ease during therapy sessions.

Overall, creating a sacred space is an essential aspect of witchcraft therapy that can help individuals feel more comfortable, safe, and supported during therapy sessions. Through the use of practices such as smudging, altars, sound healing, guided imagery, and sacred objects, individuals can create a sacred space that reflects their intention and promotes healing, growth, and self-exploration. By working with a practitioner of witchcraft therapy, individuals can develop a personalized approach to creating a sacred space that suits their unique needs and preferences.

Choosing and consecrating tools for witchcraft therapy

Choosing and consecrating tools for witchcraft therapy is an important aspect of the practice. Tools can be used to focus intention, harness energy, and facilitate healing and growth. Through the selection and consecration of tools, individuals can create a deeper connection to the practice of witchcraft therapy and promote a greater sense of empowerment and spiritual connection.

Choosing Tools for Witchcraft Therapy

Witchcraft therapy is a method that connects people with the divine and the natural world in order to promote personal development and healing. There are a several common tools and materials that practitioners frequently utilize in their practice, despite the fact that there is no one-size-fits-all approach to witchcraft therapy. In this section, we'll look at some of the witchcraft therapy's most popular tools and how they might help people grow and heal.

Altar

A witchcraft therapy practice's focal point is an altar, where practitioners can direct their energy and intention and establish a connection with the divine. An altar can be as simple or elaborate as the practitioner desires, and can include items such as candles, crystals, incense, and statues or images of deities. The altar should be kept clean and tidy, and should be a place of reverence and respect.

Candles

Candles are often used in witchcraft therapy to represent the element of fire, and to provide a focal point for meditation and ritual. Different colors of candles can be used to represent different intentions or energies, such as red for passion, green for abundance, or blue for peace. Candles can be lit during meditation or ritual, or used in spellwork to amplify intentions.

Crystals

Crystals are natural stones that are believed to have healing properties, and are often used in witchcraft therapy to support personal growth and healing. Different crystals are believed to have different properties, such as amethyst for spiritual growth, rose quartz for emotional healing, or citrine for abundance. Crystals can be worn as jewelry, carried in a pocket or pouch, or placed on an altar or in a sacred space.

Tarot Cards

Tarot cards are a tool for divination and guidance, and are widely used in witchcraft treatment to obtain insight into personal concerns and challenges. Each card has a different significance and symbolism, and can be read in many ways depending on the practitioner and the scenario. Tarot readings can be performed for oneself or another, and they can offer direction and clarity during uncertain or confusing times.

Herbs

Herbs are organic plants with medicinal and magical qualities that are frequently utilized in witchcraft therapy. As an example, lavender is said to promote relaxation while chamomile promotes sleep and sage is thought to be purifying. There are several methods to use herbs, including as incense, baths, and teas.

Athame

An athame is a ritual knife that is often used in witchcraft therapy to represent the element of air, and to direct energy and intention. An athame often features a black handle and a double-edged blade. In rituals, it is utilized to create a circle, focus energy, and expel harmful forces.

Wand

In witchcraft therapy, a wand is a tool that is used to focus energy and intention, as well as to amplify magical workings. Wands can be crafted from a variety of materials, including metal, wood, and crystal, and they can be decorated with inscriptions or symbols. Wands are frequently employed in ritual and spellwork. They can be used to direct energy, create symbols or sigils in the air, or bless items.

Bells

In witchcraft therapy, bells are frequently used to symbolize the element of air, as well as to cleanse and guard sacred spaces. The ringing of a bell is used in rituals and meditation to promote serenity and calm because it is said to disperse bad energy and purify an area.

Pendulum

A pendulum is a tool used in divination, and is often used in witchcraft therapy to gain insight and guidance. A pendulum is a weight attached to a chain or string, and is held over a surface such as a table or chart. The practitioner asks yes or no questions, and the pendulum swings in response, indicating the answer.

Book of Shadows

A Book of Shadows is a personal journal used by witches to record their experiences, spells, rituals, and other aspects of their practice. It can also include information about deities, herbs, crystals, and other tools used in witchcraft therapy. The Book of Shadows is a highly personal and private document, and is often passed down through generations of witches.

Incense

Incense is a fragrant substance that is often burned in witchcraft therapy to purify and cleanse a space, and to create a calming and sacred atmosphere. Different scents are believed to have different properties, such as lavender for relaxation, sandalwood for purification, or frankincense for protection.

Cauldron

Large metal pots called cauldrons are frequently used in witchcraft therapy to symbolize the water element and to hold fires for rituals and spellwork. Cauldrons can be used to make brews and potions, hold candles or plants, or burn incense.

Witchcraft therapy utilizes a wide range of instruments, all of which can be customized to the needs and tastes of the specific practitioner. Some practitioners might use every tool mentioned above, while others might just use a handful or even develop their own unique tools and methods. The practitioner's aim, energy, and readiness to connect with the divine and the natural world for personal growth and healing are the most crucial components of witchcraft therapy.

Consecrating Tools for Witchcraft Therapy

In witchcraft therapy, tools are often used to channel energy and intention, and to create a sacred space for personal growth and healing. These tools can include crystals, candles, tarot cards, wands, athames, and many others. To enhance the power and effectiveness of these tools, it is common practice to consecrate them, or to imbue them with positive energy and intention.

Consecration is a ritual process that involves cleansing, charging, and dedicating the tool to a specific purpose.

This process is often performed before using a new tool, or when a tool has not been used for some time. The following are some common methods for consecrating tools in witchcraft therapy.

Cleansing

The first step in consecrating a tool is to cleanse it of any negative or unwanted energies that may be present. This can be done using various methods, such as smudging with sage, purifying with salt, or washing with water. The cleansing process should be done with intention, and with the belief that the tool is being purified and made ready for its intended purpose.

Charging

After the tool has been cleansed, the next step is to charge it with positive energy and intention. This can be done by holding the tool in your hands, and visualizing a bright white light surrounding it, or by placing the tool in the sunlight or moonlight to absorb positive energy. Charging can also be done through spoken words, such as reciting a chant or prayer, or by playing music or singing over the tool.

Dedicating

The final step in consecrating a tool is to dedicate it to a specific purpose or intention. This can be done through spoken words or written intentions, such as stating that the tool is being dedicated to the service of the divine, or to a specific deity or spirit. Dedicating the tool in this way imbues it with a specific purpose and energy, and helps to focus its power towards that purpose.

Elemental Consecration

Another common method for consecrating tools in witchcraft therapy is through elemental consecration. This involves invoking the four elements of earth, air, fire, and water, and consecrating the tool with their energies. For example, a crystal could be consecrated by placing it on a bed of earth, then fanning it with incense to represent air, lighting a candle to represent fire, and sprinkling it with water to represent water.

Intentional Consecration

Intentional consecration involves setting a specific intention or purpose for the tool, and imbuing it with that energy through visualization, spoken words, or ritual. For example, a wand could be consecrated for use in healing by holding it and visualizing healing energy flowing through it, or by reciting a prayer or affirmation that affirms its intended purpose.

Anointing

Anointing is a method of consecrating a tool by using oils or other substances to imbue it with positive energy and intention. This can be done by anointing the tool with a specific oil, such as lavender for relaxation, or rosemary for purification, or by creating a special blend of oils that align with the intended purpose of the tool.

Overall, consecrating tools in witchcraft therapy is a powerful and important process that helps to focus their energy and intention towards specific purposes. There are many different methods and techniques for consecrating tools, and practitioners should choose the methods that resonate with them and their specific practice. By consecrating their tools, practitioners can enhance their effectiveness and potency, and create a stronger connection to the natural world and the divine.

Preparing yourself for witchcraft therapy

Preparing yourself for witchcraft therapy is an essential step in the process of healing and personal growth. Witchcraft therapy can be a powerful tool for exploring your emotions and experiences, but it requires a certain level of preparation, openness, and willingness to engage with the practice. You can take the following actions to get ready for witchcraft therapy:

1. Set Your Intention

By deciding what you want your practice to help you achieve and directing your energy and attention there, you may set your intention. There are several ways to accomplish this, including through journaling, meditation, or visualization. Here are some pointers and methods for focusing your intention during witchcraft therapy.
Identify your goal

Determine the goals you have for your practice as the first stage in creating your intention. This could be a specific objective like recovering from a past trauma or it could be a general intention like developing self-acceptance and love. Spend some time thinking about your practice's objectives, and then list them in a journal or on a piece of paper.

Visualize your intention

Visualizing your intention can help to bring it to life and make it more tangible. Close your eyes and sit in a serene area. Then, focus as closely as you can on your desired outcome. Think about how it would feel to accomplish your objective and how your life might change afterward. This visualization can help you stay motivated, stay focused, and focus your energy in the direction of your objective.

Write a statement of intention

Your goal may become more clear and powerful if you put it in writing. Write a short, concise sentence that accurately describes your objective, such as "I am overcoming my past trauma and cultivating self-love and acceptance." You can repeat this remark before starting any ritual or exercise to keep your goal in mind.

Use affirmations

Affirmations are positive statements that can help to reprogram your subconscious mind and align your energy towards your goal. Select a few affirmations that go along with your aim, such as "I am strong and capable of healing," or "I am worthy of love and acceptance." You can either say these affirmations out loud to yourself throughout the day or write them down and post them somewhere visible so that you can see them.

Create a sacred space

Establishing a sacred environment can improve the efficacy of your practice and promote serenity and attention. Pick a place that is peaceful and inviting where you can practice uninterrupted, and personalize it with candles, crystals, or plants that have special importance to you. This area should represent your intentions and foster a sense of communion with the divine and the natural world.

Practice meditation

Meditation is a powerful tool for creating focus and clarity, and can help to align your energy towards your intention.

Spend a few minutes each day meditating while paying attention to your breath and visualizing the outcome you want. This exercise can help you clear your thoughts, find inner peace, and direct your energy in the direction of your desire.

2. Educate Yourself

Reading books and articles, going to workshops and seminars, and picking up the knowledge of seasoned practitioners are all part of educating oneself about witchcraft. Here are some advice and methods for learning more about witchcraft in order to be prepared for witchcraft therapy.

Read books and articles

One of the finest ways to learn about witchcraft is to read books and articles. Select publications that address a variety of subjects, such as the witchcraft's history, the fundamentals of magic and ritual, and particular methods and procedures. There are many great books available on the subject, including "Witchcraft Today" by Gerald Gardner, "Drawing Down the Moon" by Margot Adler, and "The Witch's Book of Shadows" by Phyllis Curott.

Attend workshops and seminars

Another excellent option to educate yourself about witchcraft is to attend workshops and lectures. Attend online conferences and webinars or look for local workshops and seminars. These gatherings can foster a sense of community and connection while offering insightful advice from knowledgeable practitioners.

Find a mentor

Finding a mentor might be a helpful strategy for expanding your knowledge of witchcraft. Find seasoned professionals in your neighborhood, or connect with them online through social media or discussion boards. A mentor can aid with advice and support, as well as with questions and practice-related criticism.

Practice mindfulness

The effectiveness of your practice can be improved and your connection to the divine and the natural world can be deepened by engaging in mindfulness practices. Take time each day to connect with nature, whether by taking a walk in the woods, sitting by a river, or simply spending time in your garden. Allow yourself to be completely present in the moment as you pay attention to the sights, sounds, and fragrances around you.

Learn about different traditions

With many various traditions and methods, witchcraft is a broad and varied practice. Explore the similarities and distinctions across many traditions, such as Wicca, Shamanism, and Hoodoo, by taking the time to study about them. This can aid in deepening your understanding of witchcraft and offer a greater variety of methods and strategies for your own practice.

Keep an open mind

Finally, it's critical to approach your study of witchcraft with an open mind. You should keep in mind that each person's journey is unique and that there is no one "right" approach to practice. Accept other viewpoints and methods, and give oneself permission to be receptive to fresh insights and encounters. This can help to create a sense of curiosity and exploration, and can help to deepen your understanding of witchcraft and its potential for personal growth and healing.

3. Reflect on Your Emotions

Emotional awareness is a crucial component of witchcraft therapy. It's crucial to consider your emotions and gain a deeper understanding of the reasons behind them in order to use witchcraft as a therapeutic tool for personal improvement. By reflecting, you can strengthen your connection to your inner self and discover habits and behaviors that might be preventing you from moving forward.

When you reflect on your feelings, you should give yourself enough time to recognize and accept those sensations, as well as investigate the reasons behind them. This can be accomplished by a variety of activities, such as keeping a journal, meditating, or having a conversation with a therapist. In preparation for your witchcraft therapy session, we have compiled a list of some helpful advice and practices for reflecting on your feelings.

Practice mindfulness

Practicing mindfulness can help to create a sense of calm and clarity, and can help to enhance your emotional awareness. Set aside some time every day to sit in stillness and thought, bringing your attention to the sensations in your body, particularly your breath. Your thoughts and feelings will come and go regardless of whether you judge them or try to stop them.

Keep a journal

Keeping a journal is an effective method for gaining insight into one's feelings as well as recognizing recurring patterns and behaviors. Record your daily emotions in a journal, then investigate the underlying factors that contribute to them. This can assist in developing a greater sense of self-awareness and in locating potential areas for personal development and healing.

Talk with a therapist

Talking with a therapist is another valuable way to reflect on your emotions and gain deeper insight into their underlying causes. A therapist can provide a safe and supportive space for exploring your emotions, and can help to identify patterns and behaviors that may be holding you back.

Use divination tools

Divination tools, such as tarot cards or runes, can be a powerful way to reflect on your emotions and gain deeper insight into their underlying causes. Use these tools to ask questions about your emotions, and explore the symbolism and meanings behind the cards or runes.

Practice self-compassion

Practicing self-compassion is a crucial component of emotional reflection. Be gentle and kind with yourself, and allow yourself to feel your emotions without judgment or criticism. Remember that emotions are a natural part of the human experience, and that they are not good or bad, but simply are.

Identify triggers

Identifying triggers can help to create a sense of emotional awareness, and can help to avoid situations that may be emotionally challenging. Take time to reflect on situations or people that trigger strong emotional responses, and explore their underlying causes. This can help to create a sense of empowerment, and can help to develop strategies for managing difficult emotions.

4. Practice Self-Care

Self-care is a vital aspect of preparing yourself for witchcraft therapy. Practicing self-care, also known as self-nurturing, entails taking actions that are beneficial to one's physical, emotional, and spiritual well-being, and it can contribute to the development of a sense of equilibrium and stability in one's life. This, in turn, can make your practice more successful, and it can also serve to encourage personal growth and healing. In order to get ready for witchcraft therapy, the following is a list of some tips and tactics for engaging in self-care practices.

Prioritize rest and sleep

Rest and sleep are crucial for physical and emotional well-being. Prioritize getting enough sleep each night, and try to develop a regular sleep schedule. This can increase energy levels, lessen tension, and foster a peaceful state of mind.

Nourish your body

Physical and emotional wellness depend on feeding your body nutritious foods and staying hydrated. Be sure to consume a balanced diet that is high in fruits, vegetables, and whole grains. You should also drink lots of water to stay hydrated throughout the day.

Practice movement and exercise

Exercise and movement are crucial for physical health and can be beneficial for emotional wellbeing. Choose an activity you enjoy, like yoga, walking, or dancing, and work it into your daily schedule.

Establish boundaries

Establishing boundaries is crucial for emotional and spiritual well-being. Set time and energy restrictions and get comfortable saying "no" to requests or activities that don't promote your well-being. This may lessen tension and promote a feeling of empowerment.

Engage in self-care practices

Self-care activities like journaling, meditation, or taking a soothing bath can support mental, emotional, and spiritual health. Spend some time each day doing self-care activities that will leave you feeling peaceful, balanced, and centered.

Connect with nature

An effective technique to support one's emotional and spiritual wellbeing is by connecting with nature. Spend time outdoors, whether by taking a walk in the woods or simply sitting outside and observing the natural world. This may promote serenity and a sense of connectedness to nature.

Engage in creative activities

Painting, writing, or musical performance are examples of creative activities that can be used to foster emotional and spiritual well-being. Find a creative outlet you like, and schedule time each week to practice it.

Seek support

One of the most important parts of self-care can be asking for assistance from friends, family, or a therapist. When you require assistance, ask for it and accept the support and concern of others.

5. Be Open to the Experience

One of the most important steps in preparation for witchcraft therapy is to be open to the experience. Witchcraft therapy involves exploring and establishing connections with the spiritual world, which may be unfamiliar territory for some individuals. Being open to the experience can help to create a sense of receptivity and curiosity, and can help to enhance the effectiveness of your practice. Here are a few pointers and methods for becoming receptive to the experience of witchcraft therapy.

Let go of preconceived notions

It can be beneficial to let rid of preconceived ideas about witchcraft and spirituality in order to cultivate an openness and receptivity. Avoid presuming what you'll feel or how your practice will turn out; instead, go into the experience with an open heart and mind.

Embrace the unknown

Openness and curiosity can be powerfully encouraged by embracing the unknown. Accept the fact that you might not be sure what to expect from your practice and engage in its uncertainty and mystery.

Be present in the moment

A sense of connectedness and openness to the spiritual world can be facilitated by being present in the moment. Focus on the current moment instead of getting drawn into ideas about the past or the future.

Cultivate a sense of curiosity

Openness and receptivity can be fostered by developing a feeling of curiosity. Explore each experience with curiosity and intrigue as you approach your practice with wonder and interest.

Release expectations

Expectations might hinder the development of an open and receptive mindset. Avoid setting goals or expectations for your practice, and go into each encounter with an open mind and a curiosity about what may happen.

Trust the process

A feeling of openness and comfort can be produced by having faith in the process. You should have trust that the spiritual world will lead you in your practice and give yourself over to it.

Let yourself be vulnerable

Making yourself vulnerable can be a potent tool for encouraging receptivity and openness. Be willing to lower your guard and make yourself vulnerable so that you can completely engage in each encounter.

6. Set Boundaries

Establishing boundaries is a crucial part of getting ready for witchcraft therapy. Boundaries can support emotional and spiritual well-being by fostering feelings of safety, security, and empowerment. Setting limits in witchcraft therapy can help to protect your energy, foster clarity and focus, and encourage a sense of empowerment. Here are some guidelines and methods for establishing boundaries in preparation of witchcraft therapy.

Identify your boundaries

Identifying your boundaries is the first step towards setting them. To do this, consider your values, needs, and priorities and decide what matters most to you in your profession. This might assist you in identifying situations, such as ones involving relationships, the workplace, or everyday routines, where you might need to establish limits.

Communicate your boundaries

It's crucial to make your boundaries obvious to others once you've determined them. Setting clear expectations, conveying your desires and priorities, and assertively communicating your limits and boundaries are some examples of how to do this.

Honor your boundaries

Setting boundaries is only effective if you honor them consistently. This involves protecting your limits by taking action, even if it's challenging or inconvenient to do so. This may entail refusing requests that do not respect your limits, avoiding circumstances that make you feel stressed or anxious, and taking precautions to protect your energy and general wellbeing.

Practice self-care

Practicing self-care is an important aspect of setting boundaries. Self-care involves adopting measures to promote your mental, emotional, and spiritual health. It can also help you feel balanced and stable in your life. This could improve the efficiency of your practice and aid in fostering healing and personal development.

Seek support

Setting boundaries can be difficult, especially if you're not used to standing up for your goals and demands. Seeking support from friends, family, or a therapist can be a crucial component of setting boundaries. When you require assistance, reach out to others, and accept the care and support of others.

Adjust your boundaries as needed

Due to shifting demands and priorities, boundaries may need to be changed. A sense of balance and stability in your life can be achieved by frequently reviewing and adjusting your boundaries to make sure they are still fulfilling your needs and priorities.

7. Trust the Process

The first step in preparing for witchcraft therapy is to trust the procedure. In order to trust the process, you must give up control, let go of your expectations, and allow the spiritual world to direct your practice. You can encourage a state of relaxation and receptivity by having trust in the process, which will establish a solid foundation for your practice. The following are some tips and techniques for trusting the process in preparation for witchcraft therapy.

Surrender to the experience

Surrendering to the experience is an important aspect of trusting the process. This involves letting go of control and allowing yourself to be fully present in each moment. Surrendering to the experience can create a sense of openness and receptivity, and can help to enhance the effectiveness of your practice.

Let go of expectations

Letting go of expectations is another key component of trusting the process. This involves releasing any preconceived notions about what your practice should look like or what outcomes you hope to achieve. By letting go of expectations, you can create space for the spiritual realm to guide your practice, and can allow yourself to be open to new experiences and possibilities.

Cultivate a sense of curiosity

Cultivating a sense of curiosity can help to promote trust in the process. This involves approaching your practice with a sense of wonder and interest, and exploring each experience with a sense of curiosity and intrigue. By cultivating curiosity, you can create a sense of openness and receptivity, and can allow the spiritual realm to guide your practice.

Practice mindfulness

Practicing mindfulness can help to promote trust in the process. Mindfulness involves paying attention to the present moment, without judgment or distraction. You can cultivate a sense of presence and awareness as well as the capacity to fully engage in each experience by engaging in mindfulness practices.

Seek support

Seeking support from others can be an important component of trusting the process. This can involve seeking guidance or mentorship from an experienced practitioner, or simply reaching out to friends and loved ones for support and encouragement. By seeking support, you can create a sense of community and connection, and can feel more confident in your practice.

Practice self-compassion

Practicing self-compassion is another key component of trusting the process. This involves treating yourself with kindness and understanding, and acknowledging that growth and healing are often non-linear and unpredictable. You can develop a sense of acceptance and understanding as well as the ability to be patient and kind with yourself as you move through the process by engaging in self-compassion.

8. Clear Your Energy

In order to get ready for witchcraft therapy, clearing your energy is a crucial step. By letting go of any unfavorable feelings or energy that might be preventing your spiritual development and healing, you can clear your energy. You may encourage a state of openness and receptivity and establish a solid basis for your practice by clearing your energy. Here are some suggestions and methods for clearing your energy in preparation of receiving witchcraft therapy.

Practice grounding

Grounding is an important aspect of clearing your energy. Connecting with the earth through grounding can help in letting go of any excess energy or emotions that might be hindering your spiritual development. This can involve spending time in nature, visualizing roots extending from your body into the earth, or practicing yoga or meditation.

Release negative emotions

Releasing negative emotions is another key component of clearing your energy. Negative emotions can create blocks in your energy field, and can prevent you from fully engaging in your practice. This can involve practicing emotional release techniques, such as journaling, talking to a therapist, or practicing mindfulness meditation.

Cleanse your space

Cleansing your space is an important component of clearing your energy. A cluttered or chaotic environment can create blocks in your energy field, and can prevent you from fully engaging in your practice. This can involve physically cleaning your space, smudging with sage or palo santo, or using crystals or essential oils to create a sense of calm and clarity.

Practice breathwork

Practicing breathwork can help to clear your energy and promote a sense of calm and balance. Breathwork involves using the breath to release tension and promote relaxation, and can help to release any negative energy or emotions that may be blocking your spiritual growth. Pranayama or alternate nostril breathing are the examples of deep breathing exercises that can be used for this.

Use visualization techniques

Utilizing visualization techniques can be a powerful approach to free up energy and encourage calm and clarity. You can do this by seeing an energetic field or bright light around your body, or by picturing any negative energy or emotions leaving your body with each exhalation.

Set boundaries

Setting boundaries is another important aspect of clearing your energy. Boundaries can prevent unfavorable energy or emotions from entering your energy field and serve to foster a sense of safety and security. Setting clear expectations, conveying your needs and priorities, and assertively communicating your limits and boundaries are some ways of how to do this.

9. Practice Mindfulness

The first step in getting ready for witchcraft therapy is to start practicing mindfulness. Mindfulness involves paying attention to the present moment, without judgment or distraction. You can cultivate a sense of presence and awareness as well as the capacity to fully engage in each experience by engaging in mindfulness practices. The following are some advice and methods for preparing for witchcraft therapy by practicing mindfulness.

Practice breath awareness

Breath awareness is a straightforward but effective mindfulness technique that can support the development of serenity and presence. This involves concentrating on your breathing and observing the sensation of the breath entering and leaving your body. You may educate your mind to be attentive and present in each moment by engaging in breath awareness exercises, which will also help you build a solid practice base.

Use your senses

Using your senses is another effective way to practice mindfulness. This involves focusing your attention on the sensory experience of each moment, and noticing the sights, sounds, smells, tastes, and sensations around you. You can cultivate a sense of presence and awareness and enable yourself to fully engage in each event by employing your senses.

Practice body awareness

Body awareness is another important aspect of mindfulness. This is being aware of the physical feelings in your body and identifying any areas of stress, discomfort, or tightness. You can gain a better understanding of your physical and emotional state and learn to respond to your body's demands with more awareness and compassion by engaging in body awareness exercises.

Cultivate a non-judgmental attitude

Cultivating a non-judgmental attitude is another key component of mindfulness. This involves embracing each experience exactly as it is and witnessing each experience without passing judgment or criticism. You can enable yourself to fully engage in each experience while avoiding being emotionally invested in any particular result or expectation by practicing a non-judgmental attitude.

Practice gratitude

Practicing gratitude is another effective way to cultivate mindfulness. This involves focusing your attention on the positive aspects of each experience, and expressing gratitude for the blessings in your life. By practicing gratitude, you can cultivate a sense of positivity and abundance, and can create a strong foundation for your practice.

Set aside time for formal practice

Setting aside time for formal practice is an important aspect of cultivating mindfulness. This can involve practicing meditation, yoga, or other formal mindfulness practices, and dedicating a specific time each day to focus on your practice. By setting aside time for formal practice, you can create a sense of routine and consistency, and can deepen your understanding and experience of mindfulness.

10. Set Aside Distractions

When preparing for witchcraft therapy, it's important to set aside distractions in order to fully engage in the experience. Distractions can interfere with your ability to be present and fully engage in the practice, and can prevent you from getting the most out of the therapy session. Here are some tips for eliminating interruptions and establishing a concentrated setting for witchcraft therapy.

Choose a quiet, comfortable space

For distraction-free witchcraft therapy, having a peaceful, cozy atmosphere is crucial. Select a location that is free from interruptions, noise, and other distractions. This could be a specific area in your home or a peaceful outdoor setting where you can concentrate without interruptions.

Turn off electronic devices

Another crucial step in eliminating distractions is turning off technological gadgets. This entails switching off any electronic gadgets, such as your computer, phone, and others, that can distract you during the therapy session. You may completely participate in the practice and develop a sense of attention and presence by turning off all electronic gadgets.

Let others know you are unavailable

Letting others know that you are unavailable during the therapy session is another important step in setting aside distractions. Informing your family, roommates, or any other members of your household that you are not to be bothered during the treatment session is part of this. You may cultivate a sense of attention and present and keep outside distractions from interfering with the experience by establishing clear boundaries and articulating your needs.

Create a ritual or routine

Making a ritual or habit can help you block out distractions while receiving witchcraft therapy. Creating a sense of presence and focus can be achieved by using candles, burning incense, or any other practices. You can tell your mind and body when to start practicing by developing a ritual or routine, which also gives your practice a sense of continuity and consistency.

Practice mindfulness

Another efficient method for putting distractions aside during witchcraft therapy is to practice mindfulness. This involves focusing your attention on the present moment, without judgment or distraction, and allowing yourself to fully engage in the experience. You can cultivate a sense of presence and awareness and keep distractions from interfering with your ability to fully participate in the treatment session by engaging in mindfulness practices.

Set intentions and goals

Another essential step in avoiding distractions is to create intentions and goals for the treatment session. In order to do this, you must first decide why you are practicing and then establish specific objectives for each session. Setting intentions and goals enables you to establish a sense of direction and purpose while preventing interruptions from hindering you from participating fully in the therapy session.

11. Be Honest and Open

Be open and honest about your thoughts, feelings, and experiences as you get ready for witchcraft therapy. This means being willing to share your innermost thoughts and emotions with your therapist, and being open to receiving feedback and guidance. Here are some ideas for being open and truthful throughout witchcraft therapy.

Build trust with your therapist

Being open and honest during witchcraft therapy depends on developing trust with your therapist. This entails locating a therapist that you feel at ease with and who you can rely on to offer direction and support. You may create a secure and encouraging environment where you feel comfortable sharing your thoughts and feelings by developing trust with your therapist.

Recognize and acknowledge your emotions

Another crucial element in being honest and open throughout witchcraft therapy is identifying your emotions. This entails being willing to name and express your emotions, regardless of how challenging or awkward they may be. You can better understand yourself and your experiences by recognizing and acknowledging your emotions. You can also work through difficult emotions with the assistance of your therapist.

Be willing to share your experiences

Another crucial element in being honest and open throughout witchcraft therapy is being willing to discuss your experiences. This entails being open to discussing your previous mistakes, present difficulties, and future aspirations. You can acquire understanding and perspective by talking about your experiences, and you can work through challenging feelings and issues under the direction of your therapist.

Avoid judgment and self-criticism

Another critical component of being honest and open throughout witchcraft therapy is avoiding judgment and self-criticism. This involves being ready to accept both who you are and your life's experiences without condemnation or criticism. You can create a secure and encouraging environment where you feel comfortable expressing your thoughts and feelings and can work through difficult emotions with the help of your therapist by avoiding judgment and self-criticism.

Embrace vulnerability

Being honest and genuine throughout witchcraft therapy also requires embracing vulnerability. This means being willing to be vulnerable and open with your therapist, and to share your innermost thoughts and feelings without fear of judgment or rejection. By embracing vulnerability, you can gain insight and perspective, and can work through challenging emotions with the guidance of your therapist.

Practice active listening

Practicing active listening is another important step in being honest and open during witchcraft therapy. This means being willing to listen to your therapist's feedback and guidance, and to actively engage in the therapy process. By practicing active listening, you can gain insight and perspective, and can work through challenging emotions with the guidance of your therapist.

In conclusion, preparing yourself for witchcraft therapy is an essential step in the process of healing and personal growth. By setting an intention, educating yourself, reflecting on your emotions, practicing self-care, being open to the experience, setting boundaries, trusting the process, clearing your energy, practicing mindfulness, setting aside distractions, and being honest and open, you can create a safe and supportive environment for the therapy session and promote deeper insights and healing. Witchcraft therapy may be a potent tool for healing from past trauma, fostering growth and self-discovery, and exploring your emotions if you go into it with the right mindset and preparation.

The importance of intention setting in witchcraft therapy

Setting a clear and focused intention for your therapy session or practice is a crucial component of witchcraft therapy. Your therapy will be guided or focused by the intention you establish, which can assist you in getting the results you want. We'll go over what intention setting is in this section, why it's significant, and how you may use it in your witchcraft treatment practice.

What is Intention Setting?

Setting an intention entails deciding what you want to accomplish with your witchcraft treatment practice and then articulating the goal or objective. This intention can be related to a particular issue or challenge that you're facing, or to a more general desire for personal growth and development.
Your goal should be something you can actually strive toward and should be both clear and defined. For instance, your aim might be to conquer a certain obstacle

or fear, to develop a certain characteristic or trait, or to achieve a particular objective or result.

Why is Intention Setting Important?

For a number of reasons, intention setting is crucial in witchcraft therapy. First of all, it aids in giving your treatment practice emphasis and direction. You may make sure that your therapy sessions are fruitful and meaningful and that you're working toward a particular objective by establishing a clear intention.
Setting intentions can also help you become more motivated and dedicated to your treatment practice. By identifying a clear goal or outcome that you want to achieve, you can feel more motivated to put in the time and effort needed to achieve it.

Third, setting intentions can improve the effectiveness of your treatment practice. By establishing a clear intention, you may direct your concentration on the particular outcome or objective you wish to achieve and work towards it in a methodical and concentrated manner.

How to Incorporate Intention Setting into Your Witchcraft Therapy Practice

Intention setting can be included in a variety of ways within your witchcraft treatment practice. Here are some suggestions to get you started:

1. *Reflect on your goals and desires*

Start by thinking about your objectives and aims in order to have a clear intention for your witchcraft therapy practice. Think about the objectives you have for your treatment practice and the precise results or targets you wish to pursue.

2. Write down your intention

Once you've identified your intention, write it down in a clear and specific way. Be sure to articulate your intention in a way that is achievable and measurable, so that you can track your progress over time.

3. Incorporate your intention into your practice

Incorporate your intention into your witchcraft therapy practice in a tangible way. For example, you might create a ritual or spell that is focused on your intention, or you might incorporate specific practices or exercises that are designed to help you achieve your goal.

4. Use visualization and affirmation techniques

Visualization and affirmation techniques can be powerful tools for setting and achieving intentions in witchcraft therapy. Spend time visualizing yourself achieving your goal, and use affirmations to reinforce your commitment to your intention.

5. Monitor your progress

As you work towards your intention, be sure to monitor your progress and adjust your approach as needed. Regularly check in with yourself to see how you're doing, and make any necessary changes to your practice to help you stay on track.

6. *Use a physical object to represent your intention*

Choose a physical object that represents your intention, such as a crystal or a piece of jewelry, and use it as a visual reminder of your goal. You can carry the object with you or place it in a prominent location in your home or workspace to help keep your intention at the forefront of your mind.

7. Choose a mantra or affirmation

Choose a mantra or affirmation that reinforces your intention and use it as a daily reminder of your goal. Repeat the mantra or affirmation to yourself throughout the day, or incorporate it into your meditation or visualization practice.

8. Work with the phases of the moon

The phases of the moon can be a powerful tool for setting and achieving intentions in witchcraft therapy. Consider working with the energy of the moon to set your intention and track your progress over the course of the lunar cycle.

9. Create a vision board

Make a vision board that embodies your aim and put it on display in a visible place. Create a visual picture of your goal and keep it in front of you at all times by using photos, phrases, and other visual representations.

10. Collaborate with a therapist or mentor

In witchcraft treatment, working with a therapist or mentor can be beneficial for setting and achieving goals. Work together with a dependable professional who can advise and encourage you as you pursue your objective.
In the end, choosing an objective that is worthwhile and reachable, and incorporating it into your practice in a way that feels real and important to you, are the keys to effective intention setting in witchcraft therapy. With patience, commitment, and a willingness to explore new approaches and techniques, you can use the power of

intention to achieve your desired outcomes and experience meaningful growth and transformation in your life.

CHAPTER III

Techniques and Practices for Witchcraft Therapy

Meditation and visualization

Meditation and visualization are powerful techniques for promoting personal growth and healing in witchcraft therapy. In these practices, you concentrate on your thoughts, feelings, and sensations while utilizing your imagination to bring up satisfying results and experiences. This section will discuss the advantages of visualization and meditation in witchcraft therapy and offer some advice on how to apply these techniques in your own practice.

What is Meditation?

The practice of meditation involves concentrating your attention on a single idea, feeling, or object with the intention of fostering calm and relaxation. There are numerous varieties of meditation, such as mindfulness meditation, loving-kindness meditation, and guided meditation. While each kind of meditation has unique advantages, they all aim to foster inner tranquility and well-being.

Meditation is a powerful tool for promoting personal growth and healing in witchcraft therapy. You can develop a greater sense of self-awareness and gain understanding of your emotions and experiences by concentrating on your thoughts, feelings, and sensations. Additionally, meditation helps ease tension and stress, encourage relaxation, and enhance the quality of sleep.

How to Practice Meditation in Witchcraft Therapy

When paired with witchcraft therapy techniques, meditation can be a particularly potent instrument for self-discovery and personal development. Including this approach in your witchcraft therapy practice can help you gain a better knowledge of who you are, connect with your inner wisdom and intuition, and create a sense of peace and tranquility whether you are new to meditation or an experienced practitioner.

Here are some tips for practicing meditation in witchcraft therapy:

1. Find a quiet, comfortable space

When practicing meditation, it is crucial to select a peaceful, comfortable area where you may relax and focus your concentration. Choose a space where you can sit or lie down comfortably, free from distractions and interruptions.

2. Set your intention

Before beginning your meditation practice, take a few moments to set your intention. This might involve visualizing a specific outcome you would like to achieve, such as increased self-awareness, emotional healing, or spiritual growth. You can also use a specific mantra or affirmation to help you stay focused and connected to your intention throughout your practice.

3. Focus on your breath

Once you have set your intention, begin your meditation practice by focusing on your breath. Take deep, slow breaths in through your nose and out through your mouth, allowing your breath to become slower and deeper with each inhalation and exhalation.

4. Use visualization techniques

Visualization is a powerful tool for meditation, and it can be particularly effective when combined with the practices of witchcraft therapy. As you focus on your breath, visualize yourself surrounded by a sphere of protective energy or imagine yourself releasing negative emotions or thoughts into a stream of flowing water.

5. Incorporate the elements

The four elements – earth, air, fire, and water – are an integral part of witchcraft therapy, and they can be incorporated into your meditation practice as well. As you meditate, visualize each element in turn, or imagine yourself surrounded by the energies of each element.

6. Use guided meditations

Guided meditations can be a helpful way to deepen your practice and explore new approaches to meditation. There are many resources available online that offer guided meditations specifically designed for witchcraft therapy, or you can create your own guided meditation script based on your personal intentions and goals.

7. Be patient and persistent

Like any new practice, it can take time and patience to develop a consistent meditation practice. Don't be discouraged if you find it difficult to quiet your mind at first – simply continue to focus on your breath and your intention, and trust that with time and practice, your meditation practice will deepen and become more meaningful.:

What is Visualization?

The art of visualization is utilizing your mind to bring up pleasant situations and feelings. Because it enables you to visualize a desired end and concentrate your energy and attention on reaching that outcome, visualization may be a potent tool for fostering personal growth and healing.

Witchcraft therapy frequently employs visualization to assist patients in overcoming unfavorable patterns or beliefs as well as to foster a sense of empowerment and self-worth. You can develop a greater sense of self-awareness and lead a happier, more fulfilled life by imagining successful outcomes and experiences.

How to Practice Visualization in Witchcraft Therapy

Visualization is a powerful instrument for personal development and change, and it can be especially successful when used in conjunction with other witchcraft therapeutic techniques. By using your imagination to create vivid mental images and harnessing the power of your mind to manifest your desires, you can unlock your full potential and create the life you truly want.

Here are some tips for practicing visualization in witchcraft therapy:

1. Choose a quiet, comfortable space

When practicing visualization, it is important to choose a quiet, comfortable space where you can relax and focus your attention. This might involve creating a special space for visualization, such as a dedicated altar or sacred area in your home, or simply finding a quiet corner where you can sit or lie down comfortably.

2. Set your intention

Before beginning your visualization practice, take a few moments to set your intention. This might involve visualizing a specific outcome you would like to achieve, such as improved self-confidence, emotional healing, or greater abundance and prosperity. Be as specific and detailed as possible when setting your intention, and use a specific mantra or affirmation to help you stay focused and connected to your goal throughout your practice.

3. Use all of your senses

When visualizing, it is important to engage all of your senses to create a vivid mental image. This might involve imagining the sights, sounds, smells, tastes, and textures of your desired outcome, or using specific symbols or images to represent your intention.

4. Incorporate the elements

The four elements – earth, air, fire, and water – are an integral part of witchcraft therapy, and they can be incorporated into your visualization practice as well. For example, you might imagine yourself surrounded by a circle of protective energy, or visualize yourself releasing negative emotions or thoughts into a stream of flowing water.

5. Use guided visualization scripts

Guided visualization scripts can be a helpful way to deepen your practice and explore new approaches to visualization. There are many resources available online that offer guided visualization scripts specifically designed for witchcraft therapy, or you can create your own guided visualization based on your personal intentions and goals.

6. Incorporate visualization into your daily routine

To maximize the benefits of visualization, it is important to incorporate it into your daily routine. This might involve practicing visualization as part of your morning or evening ritual, or visualizing your goals and intentions during meditation or other daily practices.

7. Be patient and persistent

Like any new practice, it can take time and persistence to develop a consistent visualization practice. Don't be discouraged if you find it difficult to create vivid mental images at first – simply continue to focus on your intention and engage all of your senses to bring your visualization to life.

Benefits of Meditation in Witchcraft Therapy

Meditation is a practice that has been used for thousands of years to promote physical, mental, and emotional well-being. In the context of witchcraft therapy, meditation can be a powerful tool for grounding, centering, and connecting with your inner self. Here are some of the benefits of incorporating meditation into your witchcraft therapy practice:

Cultivates mindfulness: Meditation teaches you to become consciously aware of your thoughts, feelings, and sensations without passing judgment on them. You can develop greater self-awareness and increase your sensitivity to your inner experiences by engaging in mindfulness practices.

Reduces stress and anxiety: Meditation has been demonstrated to lessen symptoms of anxiety and depression and enhance emotions of peace and relaxation. By including meditation into your witchcraft therapy practice, you can learn to handle stress and regulate your emotions more effectively.

Increases spiritual connection: Meditation can help you establish a deeper connection with the divine, the natural world, and your inner self. Regular meditation practice can strengthen your spiritual connection and help you find inner serenity and direction.

Accesses inner wisdom: Meditation can assist you in developing your intuition and inner wisdom by encouraging mental stillness and introspection. This can be particularly helpful when working through difficult emotions or making important decisions.

Benefits of Visualization in Witchcraft Therapy

Visualization is a technique that involves using your imagination to create mental images or scenes. In the context of witchcraft therapy, visualization can be a powerful tool for manifesting your desires, releasing negative emotions, and connecting with your inner self. Here are some of the benefits of incorporating visualization into your witchcraft therapy practice:

Manifests desires: Visualization can help you to clarify your goals and desires and create a mental image of what you want to manifest in your life. By focusing your intention and attention on your desired outcome, you can increase the likelihood of it coming to fruition.

Releases negative emotions: Visualization can also be used to release negative emotions such as fear, anger, and sadness. By creating a mental image of these emotions leaving your body, you can begin to let go of them and create space for more positive emotions to emerge.

Connects with inner self: Visualization can assist you in reaching out to your inner wisdom and intuition. You can start to bring your thoughts, feelings, and actions in alignment with this vision by developing a mental image of yourself as whole, healthy, and empowered.

Enhances self-esteem: Visualization can also be used to boost self-confidence. You can start to embody these qualities in your daily routine by developing a picture of yourself that is confident and competent in your mind.

Incorporating meditation and visualization into your witchcraft therapy practice

A potent strategy to communicate with your inner self, activate your intuition, and effect positive change in your life is to incorporate meditation and visualization exercises into your witchcraft therapy routine. Meditation and visualization are practices that have been used for thousands of years in various spiritual and healing traditions, and are also widely recognized as effective tools for managing stress and anxiety.

Meditation is a practice that involves training the mind to focus on the present moment, often through the use of breathing techniques and guided imagery. Visualization, on the other hand, involves using the imagination to create vivid mental images that promote relaxation, healing, and personal growth. Together, these practices can help you to quiet your mind, access deeper levels of awareness, and develop a greater sense of inner peace and well-being.

Incorporating meditation and visualization into your witchcraft therapy practice can be done in a number of ways, depending on your preferences and needs. Here are some ideas to get you started:

Start with the basics: If you're new to meditation or visualization, it can be helpful to start with some basic techniques to get you comfortable with the practice. Simple breath-focused meditation or guided visualizations can be a great place to begin. There are many resources available online or in books that can guide you through these practices.

Make it a daily habit: Consistency is key when it comes to meditation and visualization. Try to set aside a regular time each day for your practice, even if it's just a few minutes. This can help you to establish a routine and make it easier to stick to your practice.

Create a dedicated space: Designate a space in your home that feels calm and peaceful, and use it as your meditation and visualization space. This can help you to create a sense of sacredness around your practice and make it easier to focus.

Use props and tools: There are many props and tools that can enhance your meditation and visualization practice. Some people like to use candles, incense, or crystals to create a soothing atmosphere. Others prefer to use guided meditations or visualization scripts.

Set an intention: Before you begin your practice, take a moment to set an intention for what you hope to achieve. This can help you to focus your mind and direct your energy toward a specific goal.
Incorporate movement: Movement can be a powerful way to enhance your meditation and visualization practice. You might try incorporating gentle yoga poses or stretches, or simply taking a mindful walk in nature.
Practice gratitude: Gratitude is a powerful emotion that can help to cultivate feelings of joy and contentment. Consider incorporating a gratitude practice into your meditation and visualization routine by taking a few moments to reflect on what you're thankful for each day.

Overall, meditation and visualization are powerful techniques for promoting personal growth and healing in witchcraft therapy. By practicing these techniques, you can cultivate a deeper sense of self-awareness, reduce stress and anxiety, promote relaxation, and create positive outcomes and experiences. To incorporate meditation and visualization into your witchcraft therapy practice, it is important to set clear intentions, focus your attention, and practice regularly. These techniques can be incorporated into your witchcraft treatment sessions to improve your experience and encourage more profound healing and personal development.

Spellwork and ritual

Spellwork and ritual are powerful tools for promoting personal growth and healing in witchcraft therapy. These rituals involves the use of occult symbols, incantations, and hand gestures to direct your intention and energy toward a particular outcome. This section will discuss the advantages of spellwork and ritual in witchcraft therapy and offer advice on how to utilize these techniques in your own practice.

What is Spellwork?

Spellwork is the art of directing your energy and purpose toward a certain objective or result by employing symbolic objects, incantations, and gestures. Candles, crystals, herbs, and other items can be used in spells to manifest your intention physically. They may also involve reciting incantations, performing gestures, or engaging in other ritual actions to enhance the power of your intention.

In witchcraft therapy, spellwork is a potent technique for encouraging healing and personal development. You can develop a stronger sense of intention and purpose by making a physical representation of your aim and employing ritual actions to focus your energy. Spellwork can also help you strengthen the impact of your intention and bring your conscious and unconscious thoughts into harmony.

How to Practice Spellwork in Witchcraft Therapy

Spellwork is a potent tool for channelling the universal energy and bringing about favourable change in your life. Spellwork can be a powerful tool for achieving your objectives and achieving your complete potential, whether you're looking for emotional healing, financial abundance, or increased self-awareness. The following are some pointers for casting spells in magical therapy:

1. Choose your intention

It's crucial to decide on your purpose before casting any spells. This might involve setting a specific goal or desire that you would like to manifest, such as improved health, increased prosperity, or greater spiritual connection. When choosing your intention, be as precise and detailed as you can. Throughout your practice, use positive affirmations and representations to help you remain focused and connected to your goal.

2. Gather your tools

Depending on the kind of spell you are crafting and your particular preferences, a wide variety of tools and materials can be used in spellwork. In addition to more conventional objects like wands, athames, and cauldrons, common instruments include candles, herbs, crystals, and essential oils. Select resources that support your purpose and assist you in concentrating your energy and intention.

3. Prepare your space

Making a sacred space is crucial to spellwork because it enables you to connect with the universe and concentrate on your purpose. In your home, you might do this by creating an altar or a sacred place, or you might just clear a spot where you can sit or stand comfortably and concentrate your energy.

4. Cast your circle

By casting a circle, you can surround yourself and your area with protection and increase the vitality of your spellwork. This could entail visualising a protective energy sphere encircling you and your space, using particular words or symbols, or both.

5. Focus your energy and intention

It's time to direct your energy and purpose towards achieving your goal after you've set your intention, gathered your tools, and prepared your environment. This might entail focusing your energy and purpose by reciting affirmations or spells that assist you in doing so, or using visualization techniques to visualise the result you want.

6. Release your energy into the universe

Once you have focused your energy and intention on your goal, it is important to release your energy into the universe and trust that it will be returned to you in the form of positive change. This might involve blowing out a candle, releasing a symbol of your intention into the wind, or simply visualizing your intention being released into the universe.

7. Ground and center yourself

After completing any spellwork, it is important to ground and center yourself to ensure that you remain connected to the energy of the universe and maintain your focus and intention. This might involve taking a few deep breaths, meditating, or performing a grounding ritual such as walking barefoot in nature or holding a grounding crystal.
What is Ritual?

Ritual is the practice of engaging in symbolic actions or behaviors to create a sense of connection with a higher power or spiritual energy. Rituals may involve performing specific actions, such as lighting candles, reciting prayers, or engaging in meditation or visualization practices. They may also involve creating a specific atmosphere or environment, such as by using incense or other aromatherapy products.

In witchcraft therapy, ritual is a powerful tool for encouraging healing and personal development. You can develop a sense of connection with your higher self, the divine, or spiritual energy through engaging in symbolic actions or behaviors. Rituals can also support the development of intention and focus, which can improve the results of therapeutic sessions.

How to Practice Ritual in Witchcraft Therapy

Rituals play a significant role in witchcraft therapy because they help us connect with universal energy and bring about good change in our lives. Ritual practice can assist you in developing your routine and establishing a connection with your authentic self, whether you are looking to achieve emotional recovery, spiritual development, or greater self-awareness. The following advice is for performing ceremony in witchcraft therapy:

1. *Set your intention*

Setting your intention is crucial before starting any ritual. This might involve choosing a specific goal or desire that you would like to manifest, or simply focusing your attention on a particular aspect of your life that you would like to improve. When setting your intention, be as precise and detailed as you can. Throughout your practice, use uplifting affirmations and visualizations to help you remain focused and connected to your goal.

2. *Gather your tools*

Depending on your personal tastes and the kind of ritual you are performing, a wide variety of tools and materials can be used. Candles, crystals, herbs, and essential oils are typical instruments, along with more conventional objects like wands, athames, and cauldrons. Select resources that support your purpose and assist you in concentrating your energy and intention.

3. Prepare your space

Creating a sacred space is an important part of ritual, as it allows you to connect with the energy of the universe and focus your attention on your intention. In the place you live, you might do this by creating an altar or a sacred place, or you might just clear an area where you can sit or stand comfortably and concentrate your energy.

4. Cast your circle

Creating a protective barrier around yourself and your space by casting a circle is one way to do so, and doing so can also help to amplify the energy of the ceremony you are performing. This could involve using particular words or symbols to cast your circle, or it could simply involve envisioning a protective sphere of energy surrounding both you and the place you are in.

5. Call upon the elements

Through the use of the elements, you can invoke the strength and support of the universe's energies for your ceremony. You could do this by concentrating on the energies of the universe and asking them to direct and support you in your practice, or you might call on the elements of earth, air, fire, and water.

6. Perform your ritual

Once you have set your intention, gathered your tools, prepared your space, cast your circle, and called upon the elements, it is time to perform your ritual. This might involve reciting specific words or chants, using visualization techniques to create a mental image of your desired outcome, or simply focusing your energy and intention on your goal.

7. Release your energy into the universe

After completing your ritual, it is important to release your energy into the universe and trust that it will be returned to you in the form of positive change. This might involve blowing out a candle, releasing a symbol of your intention into the wind, or simply visualizing your intention being released into the universe.

8. Ground and center yourself

After practicing ritual, it is important to ground and center yourself to ensure that you remain connected to the energy of the universe and maintain your focus and intention. This might involve taking a few deep breaths, meditating, or performing a grounding ritual such as walking barefoot in nature or holding a grounding crystal.

Benefits of spellwork and rituals in witchcraft therapy

Fostering Connection with the Divine

One of the primary benefits of spellwork and rituals in witchcraft therapy is their ability to foster a connection with the divine. Many practitioners believe that by working with elements such as herbs, candles, and crystals, they can tap into the energies of the earth and the universe, and connect with deities and spirits. This connection can provide a sense of comfort, guidance, and support during difficult times, and can help individuals to feel more spiritually grounded and connected.

Promoting Mindfulness and Focus

Spellwork and rituals require a great deal of focus and attention to detail, which can help individuals to become more mindful and present in the moment. Practicing mindfulness has been shown to have numerous benefits, including reduced stress and anxiety, improved cognitive function, and increased emotional regulation. People who practice witchcraft therapy can develop a sense of mindfulness and focus that will help them in all aspects of their lives by incorporating spellwork and rituals.

Encouraging Personal Empowerment

The ability of spellwork and rituals to promote personal empowerment is one of the witchcraft therapy's most potent advantages. People can experience a sense of agency and control over their lives by engaging in spells and rituals that are intended to accomplish particular objectives. This can motivate people to take action and effect change, which can be particularly helpful for those who feel helpless or stuck in their present situations.

Promoting Self-Care

Witchcraft therapy uses a lot of spells and rituals that are intended to encourage self-love and self-care. For example, a ritual that involves taking a relaxing bath with herbs and oils can help individuals to feel more nurtured and cared for, while a spell for protection can help individuals to feel more secure and safe. By incorporating self-care practices into their witchcraft therapy practice, individuals can prioritize their own needs and wellbeing, and create a stronger foundation for personal growth and healing.

Fostering Creativity and Imagination

Spellwork and rituals are highly creative practices, and require individuals to use their imaginations to visualize and manifest their intentions. This can be a powerful tool for individuals who struggle with creativity or imagination in other areas of their lives. By engaging in spellwork and rituals, individuals can strengthen their creative muscles, and learn to think outside of the box to find solutions to problems.

Cultivating a Sense of Community

Finally, practicing spellwork and rituals in a group setting can foster a sense of community and belonging. Many witches practice in groups, and participating in group rituals and ceremonies can provide individuals with a sense of support and camaraderie. This sense of community can be especially important for individuals who feel isolated or disconnected from others in their daily lives.

Incorporating Spellwork and Rituals into Your Witchcraft Therapy Practice

Setting Your Intentions

The first step in incorporating spellwork and rituals into your witchcraft therapy practice is to set your intentions. What do you want to achieve through your practice? What areas of your life do you want to focus on? Be specific and clear about what you want to manifest.

Selecting Your Tools and Materials

Once you have set your intentions, you can select the tools and materials you will use to support your practice. This may include candles, crystals, herbs, and other ritual objects. Choose items that resonate with your intentions and that feel meaningful to you.

Creating Your Ritual or Spell

Using your intentions and selected materials as a guide, create a ritual or spell that supports your goals. This may involve writing out a specific incantation, designing a ritual structure, or selecting specific objects to use in your practice.

Engaging in Your Practice

Once you have created your ritual or spell, it's time to engage in your practice. Set aside a specific time and space for your ritual or spellwork, and take the time to fully immerse yourself in the experience. Engage all of your senses and focus your energy on your intention.

Reflecting on Your Experience

After your practice, take time to reflect on your experience. What did you learn? Did you notice any shifts or changes in your energy or perspective? Use this reflection time to deepen your self-awareness and build on your spiritual growth.

In conclusion, spellwork and ritual are powerful tools for promoting personal growth and healing in witchcraft therapy. By using symbolic objects, incantations, and gestures, you can focus your energy and intention toward a specific goal or outcome. Additionally, spellwork and ritual can help to enhance the power of your intention and create a sense of alignment between your conscious and unconscious minds. Setting clear goals, concentrating your energy, and participating in these activities frequently are essential if you want to integrate spellwork and ritual into your witchcraft therapy practice. You can improve your experience and encourage more profound healing and psychological development by doing this.

Divination and tarot reading

Witchcraft treatment uses strong tools like divination and tarot reading to encourage healing and personal development. To develop understanding of your thoughts, feelings, and experiences, these techniques involve the use of symbolic tools. In this section, we will examine the advantages of tarot reading and divination in witchcraft treatment and offer some advice on how to apply these techniques in your own practice.

What is Divination?

Using symbolic objects to obtain insight into your thoughts, feelings, and experiences is the practice of divination. Astrology, numerology, and runes are just a few examples of the many various kinds of divination. Each type of divination has its own benefits, but they all share a common goal of promoting self-awareness and understanding.

In witchcraft therapy, divination is a potent technique for encouraging healing and personal development. You can develop a greater sense of self-awareness and achieve clarity on your course of action by employing symbolic tools to acquire insight into your ideas, feelings, and experiences. A sense of empowerment and anxiety reduction are two other benefits of divination.

How to Practice Divination in Witchcraft Therapy

Using instruments and methods to predict the future, comprehend the present more fully, or understand oneself is the practice of divination. Divination can be a tool for spiritual connection, self-awareness, and personal development in witchcraft therapy. The following guidance is for using divination in witchcraft therapy:

1. Choose your tool

There are many different tools that can be used for divination, each with its own unique strengths and weaknesses. Tarot cards, oracle cards, runes, pendulums, scrying mirrors, and crystal balls are some of the instruments most frequently used in witchcraft treatment. Chose an instrument that speaks to you and that you are at ease using.

2. Get to know your tool

It's crucial to get to know your divination instrument well once you've decided on it. To develop a deeper connection and understanding with the tool, spend some time learning the symbolism and meanings of the cards or symbols and use it frequently.

3. Create a sacred space

Making a sacred place is crucial to divination because it enables you to communicate with the forces of the universe and your intuition. This may entail creating a special altar or sacred space in your living place, or it may simply involve locating a calm, serene area where you can rest and concentrate your energy.

4. Set your intention

Before beginning any divination practice, it is important to set your intention. This might involve choosing a specific question or area of your life that you would like guidance on, or simply asking for general guidance and insight. Be clear and specific when setting your intention, and use positive affirmations and visualizations to help you stay focused and connected to your goal throughout your practice.

5. Shuffle and draw your cards/symbols

Once you have set your intention and created your sacred space, it is time to shuffle your cards or symbols and draw your first card or symbol. Take your time and focus your energy on your intention as you shuffle and draw your cards/symbols, and trust that the universe will guide you to the message you need to hear.

6. Interpret the message

Once you have drawn your cards/symbols, it is time to interpret the message they are telling you. This might involve studying the symbolism and meanings of the cards/symbols, or simply allowing your intuition to guide you as you connect with the energy of the universe.

7. Take action

After interpreting the message, it is important to take action to incorporate it into your life. This might involve making specific changes or taking specific actions based on the guidance you received, or simply allowing the message to guide your thoughts and actions in a more general sense.

8. Reflect and review

It is important to take some time after your divination practice to consider the message you received and to evaluate any actions you may have taken as a result of the advice you received. This can help you to deepen your practice and gain greater insight into yourself and the world around you.

What is Tarot Reading?

In order to obtain insight into your thoughts, feelings, and experiences, a deck of cards is used in a specific type of divination called a tarot reading. Each tarot card has a specific meaning, and the cards are used to create a narrative or story that reflects your current situation.

In witchcraft therapy, tarot reading is a potent technique for promoting healing and personal development. You may establish a greater sense of self-awareness and obtain direction on your future by using tarot cards to gain insight into your thoughts, feelings, and experiences. Tarot reading can also aid in easing anxiety and fostering a sense of empowerment.

How to Practice Tarot Reading in Witchcraft Therapy

A deck of 78 cards is used in tarot readings, a common form of divination, to provide information about the past, present, and future. Tarot reading can be a potent tool for spiritual connection, self-awareness, and personal development in witchcraft therapy. Following are some pointers for tarot reading in witchcarft therapy:

1. Choose your deck

Tarot decks come in a wide variety, each with a special style and meaning. When choosing a deck, it is important to choose one that resonates with you and that you feel comfortable using. The Thoth deck, the Wild Unknown deck, and the Rider-Waite-Smith deck are a few well-known cards.

2. Get to know your deck

It's essential to familiarize yourself with your tarot cards once you've made your selection. To create a stronger bond with and comprehension of the deck, spend some time learning the symbolism and meanings of each card and practice using it frequently.

3. Create a sacred space

Tarot reading requires you to create a sacred place in order to connect with the energies of the universe and your intuition. This may entail creating a special altar or sacred space in your home, or it may simply involve locating a calm, serene area where you can rest and concentrate your energy.

4. Set your intention

Setting an intention is crucial before starting any tarot reading. This might involve choosing a specific question or area of your life that you would like guidance on, or simply asking for general guidance and insight. Be clear and specific when setting your intention, and use positive affirmations and visualizations to help you stay focused and connected to your goal throughout your practice.

5. Shuffle and draw your cards

Once you have set your intention and created your sacred space, it is time to shuffle your tarot deck and draw your cards. Take your time and focus your energy on your intention as you shuffle and draw your cards, and trust that the universe will guide you to the message you need to hear.

6. Interpret the message

Once you have drawn your cards, it is time to interpret the message they are telling you. This might involve studying the symbolism and meanings of the cards, or simply allowing your intuition to guide you as you connect with the energy of the universe.

7. Take action

After interpreting the message, it is important to take action to incorporate it into your life. This might involve making specific changes or taking specific actions based on the guidance you received, or simply allowing the message to guide your thoughts and actions in a more general sense.

8. Reflect and review

After completing your tarot reading, it is important to take some time to reflect on the message you received and review any actions you have taken based on the guidance you received. This can help you to deepen your practice and gain greater insight into yourself and the world around you.

Benefits of Divination and Tarot Reading in Witchcraft Therapy

Divination is the practice of seeking knowledge of the future or the unknown through supernatural means. Tarot reading is one of the most popular forms of divination, and is often used in witchcraft therapy as a tool for personal growth, self-awareness, and spiritual connection. Here are some of the advantages of tarot cards and divination in witchcraft therapy:

Gain insight and clarity

The ability to obtain understanding and clarity about your life is one of the main advantages of divination and tarot reading in witchcraft therapy. Tarot cards are thought to be a reflection of the subconscious mind and can disclose underlying tendencies, notions, and feelings that might be having an impact on your life. You can comprehend yourself and your situation better through divination and tarot reading, and you can gain the perspective and clarity you need to proceed.

Connect with your intuition

You can connect with your intuition and inner knowledge by using divination and tarot reading. You can learn more about your own inner voice and intuition by allowing yourself to be open and receptive to the messages of the world. This can help you to make more informed decisions, trust your instincts, and develop greater self-awareness.

Develop a deeper spiritual connection

You can strengthen your spiritual ties to the universe and the divine by using divination and tarot reading. You can acquire more knowledge, direction, and wisdom by connecting with the spiritual world and the energies of the universe. This can support you in feeling more a part of the world around you and in finding more significance and purpose in your life.

Release negative emotions

Tarot reading and divination are both effective methods for letting go of negative feelings and energy. You can let go of unfavourable ideas, beliefs, and emotions that could be limiting you by connecting with the energy of the universe and your own subconscious mind. This can promote greater personal development and healing while making you feel lighter, more energized, and more optimistic.

Identify and overcome obstacles

Through divination and tarot reading, you can also identify and overcome obstacles that may be standing in the way of your personal growth and development. You can create a strategy for overcoming obstacles and achieving your objectives by gaining understanding of your circumstances as well as your own thoughts and beliefs. You may feel more in control and assured of your ability to design the life you want as a result of this.

Develop greater self-awareness

You can improve your self-awareness and comprehension of your own thoughts, feelings, and behaviors by using divination and tarot reading. You can spot patterns, ideas, and emotions that can be preventing you from moving forward or hurting you by gaining insight into your own mind and the energy surrounding you. You may be able to change your life for the better as a result, and you may also grow more self-aware and accepting of who you are.

Improve your relationships

Divination and tarot reading can also be a powerful tool for improving your relationships with others. You can develop a deeper knowledge of others and their viewpoints by gaining more understanding of your own emotions and behaviours. This can facilitate more effective communication, conflict resolution, and the development of enduring, satisfying connections with the people in your life.

Incorporating Divination and Tarot Reading into Your Witchcraft Therapy Practice

Including divination and tarot reading in your witchcraft therapy sessions can be a very effective way to get clarity, direction, and insight on your path to healing and personal development. Here are some pointers for including tarot reading and divination in your witchcraft treatment practice:

Choose a deck that resonates with you

Tarot decks come in a wide variety, each with its own special symbolism and spirit. It's crucial to pick a deck that appeals to you and feels like a good match for your unique preferences and style when making your selection. You may want to spend some time researching different decks and reading reviews to find one that feels right for you.

Take time to connect with your deck

Before you begin using your tarot deck for divination or readings, it is important to take some time to connect with it and establish a relationship. You may want to spend some time meditating with your deck, shuffling the cards, and getting to know the symbolism and energy of each card. This can help you to establish a deeper connection with your deck and to feel more comfortable and confident using it for divination and tarot reading.

Set your intention

Before each divination or tarot reading session, it is important to set your intention and focus your energy on the question or issue that you wish to explore. You may want to spend some time meditating or reflecting on your intention before beginning your reading, and to use visualization or other techniques to help you connect with the energy of the cards and the universe.

Choose a spread that fits your intention

There are many different tarot spreads that you can use for divination and readings, each with its own unique structure and symbolism. When choosing a spread, it is important to choose one that fits your intention and that will help you to gain insight and clarity on the issue or question that you wish to explore. You may want to spend some time researching different spreads and experimenting with different layouts to find one that works best for you.

Practice self-care

Divination and tarot reading can be emotionally intense and can sometimes bring up difficult or challenging emotions. It is important to practice self-care before, during, and after your reading sessions to help you stay grounded and balanced. You may want to spend some time meditating or practicing relaxation techniques before and after your reading, and to make sure that you are in a comfortable and safe environment.

Reflect on your reading

It's crucial to take some time to think back on each divination or tarot reading experience and to journal about your revelations and insights. This can aid in your learning integration and assist you comprehend yourself and your situation better. You could also want to set aside some time to meditate, think about the reading, or utilize other methods to connect with the energies of the universe and the cards.

Seek guidance and support

If you are new to divination or tarot reading, or if you are experiencing difficult emotions or challenges, it can be helpful to seek guidance and support from a trusted practitioner or mentor. You may want to consider joining a local witchcraft or tarot reading group, or to seek out online resources and communities that can provide guidance and support.

Overall, divination and tarot reading are powerful tools for promoting personal growth and healing in witchcraft therapy. By using symbolic tools to gain insight into your thoughts, emotions, and experiences, you can cultivate a deeper sense of self-awareness and gain clarity on your path forward. Additionally, these practices can help to reduce anxiety and promote a sense of empowerment. To incorporate divination and tarot reading into your witchcraft therapy practice, it is important to set clear intentions, focus your attention, and practice regularly. By doing so, you can enhance your experience and promote deeper healing and personal growth.

Herbalism and aromatherapy

Herbalism and aromatherapy are powerful techniques for promoting personal growth and healing in witchcraft therapy. These methods improve physical, emotional, and spiritual well-being by utilizing the therapeutic benefits of plants and essential oils. This section will discuss the advantages of herbal and aromatherapy in witchcraft therapy and offer advice on how to apply these techniques in your own practice.

What is Herbalism?

Utilizing a plant's therapeutic qualities to promote one's physical, emotional, and spiritual well-being is known as herbalism. For thousands of years, people have utilized plants as medicine, and today, herbalism is still a popular type of natural medicine. Numerous illnesses, including anxiety, melancholy, sleeplessness, and chronic pain, can be treated with herbal treatments.

In witchcraft therapy, herbalism is a potent tool for encouraging healing and psychological development. By using the healing properties of plants, you can support your physical and emotional well-being and promote a deeper sense of connection to the natural world. Herbalism can also aid in calming the mind and reducing tension..

How to Practice Herbalism in Witchcraft Therapy

1. Research: It's crucial to carry out study before introducing any new herbs into your practice. Make sure the herbs you use are safe for you by learning about their qualities and uses. Be mindful of any possible interactions between prescription drugs and other medical issues.

2. Choose your Herbs: After conducting your study, select the herbs that speak to you and your objectives. Herbs can be chosen for their medicinal qualities, their symbolism, or their affinity with a certain deity or spirit.

3. Prepare your Herbs: Making herbal teas, tinctures, salves, and incense are just a few of the many ways you can get ready your herbs for use in witchcraft therapy. Research different methods and choose the one that feels right for you.

4. Include Herbs in Your Practice: After preparing your herbs, include them in your witchcraft ritual. They can be incorporated into your everyday routine or used in rituals, spellwork, and meditation.

5. Work with intention: It's crucial to use purpose when utilizing herbs in your practice. Be specific about your objectives and desired results when setting your purpose for the herb. This will assist you in maintaining mental concentration while using the herb.

6. Practice mindfulness: It's essential to pay attention to how your body responds to herbs as well as any changes in your energy or feelings. Pay attention to the effects the plant has on you and change your routine as necessary.

7. Respect the Plants: When working with plants, it's essential to be respectful and appreciative. Be mindful of your effect on the environment and thank the plant for providing you with energy and healing qualities.

What is Aromatherapy?

Aromatherapy is the practice of using essential oils to promote physical, emotional, and spiritual well-being. Plants can be used to produce essential oils, which are concentrated scents and medicines. Popular in alternative medicine, aromatherapy can be used to cure a variety of ailments, such as stress, anxiety, and depression.

In witchcraft therapy, aromatherapy is a potent technique for encouraging healing and personal development. You can encourage a stronger sense of connection to nature, lessen stress, and increase mental and physical well-being by utilizing essential oils.

How to Practice Aromatherapy in Witchcraft Therapy

Step 1: Choose your essential oils

Selecting the essential oils you'll use is the first step in using aromatherapy in witchcraft therapy. There are many different scents of essential oils, and each one has special qualities that can influence your mood, level of vitality, and general well-being. It's essential to choose oils that resonate with your intentions and needs. For example, if you're working on healing emotional wounds, you may want to choose lavender, chamomile, or frankincense essential oils.

Step 2: Choose your application method

Once you have chosen your essential oils, the next step is to decide how you want to use them. Essential oils can be applied topically, diffused in the air, or added to bathwater or massage oil. Each method has its benefits, and the choice depends on your preferences and needs. For example, if you want to promote relaxation and reduce anxiety, diffusing essential oils in the air or adding them to a bath may be most effective.

Step 3: Prepare your space

Before practicing aromatherapy in witchcraft therapy, it's essential to create a comfortable and inviting space. You may want to light candles, burn incense, or play soft music to enhance the atmosphere. You can also create a ritual around your aromatherapy practice, such as lighting a candle or saying a prayer before diffusing your oils.

Step 4: Dilute your essential oils

It's important to dilute essential oils before applying them topically. Essential oils are strong and can irritate skin when applied directly. One spoonful of carrier oil, such as almond or jojoba oil, should be added for every drop of essential oil, according to the general rule of thumb. The oil can then be applied to your skin, for example, on your wrists or temples.

Step 5: Diffuse your essential oils

The medicinal benefits of essential oils can be obtained by diffusing them. You can apply a few droplets of oil to a cotton ball or tissue, a bowl of hot water, or a diffuser. The fragrance can then be breathed in and allowed to fill the room.

Step 6: Use essential oils in massage or bath

Another way to practice aromatherapy in witchcraft therapy is to add essential oils to a massage oil or bathwater. You can mix a few drops of essential oil with a carrier oil, such as almond or coconut oil, and use it for self-massage or partner massage. Adding a few drops of essential oil to your bathwater can also help you relax and promote well-being.

Step 7: Cleanse your space

After practicing aromatherapy in witchcraft therapy, it's essential to cleanse your space to remove any negative energy or residue. You can use tools such as sage, palo santo, or incense to smudge your space and create a clean and inviting atmosphere.

Benefits of Herbalism in Witchcraft Therapy:

Physical Healing: Many herbs have potent healing properties that can help alleviate physical ailments and promote overall wellness. For example, lavender is often used to help relieve stress and anxiety, while chamomile is known for its calming effects on the body and mind. Echinacea is commonly used to support the immune system, and ginger can aid in digestion and alleviate nausea.

Emotional Healing: Herbs can also be utilized to encourage mental balance and healing. For instance, mugwort is well known for its capacity to improve intuition and dreamwork, while rose petals are frequently used in love spells and ceremonies to encourage self-love and compassion. A popular remedy for anxiety and depression symptoms is St. John's wort.

Connection to Nature: Herbalism is a means to establish a connection with the natural world and with nature. You can strengthen your connection to the earth and the seasons by incorporating herbs into your witchcraft rituals.

Spiritual Growth: Herbalism can also be an effective instrument for spiritual development and growth. You can gain a deeper understanding of yourself and your connection to the world around you by working with plants and their energies.

Benefits of Aromatherapy in Witchcraft Therapy

Aromatherapy has many benefits when incorporated into a witchcraft therapy practice. Here are some of the ways that aromatherapy can help you in your healing journey:

Promotes Relaxation: Many essential oils have a calming effect on the body and mind. They can help to reduce stress and anxiety, promote relaxation, and improve sleep quality.
Enhances Focus and Concentration: Some essential oils can help to improve focus and concentration, making them useful during meditation and visualization practices.

Eases Physical Discomfort: Certain essential oils have anti-inflammatory and analgesic properties that can help to ease physical discomfort and pain.

Supports Emotional Healing: Essential oils can help to support emotional healing by promoting feelings of calm, balance, and grounding.

Promotes Spiritual Connection: Many essential oils have a strong connection to spirituality and can help to promote a deeper sense of connection with the divine.

Incorporating Herbalism and Aromatherapy into Your Witchcraft Therapy Practice

To incorporate herbalism and aromatherapy into your witchcraft therapy practice, it is important to choose high-quality ingredients, set clear intentions, and practice regularly. You might want to include aromatherapy and herbalism in your everyday self-care routine or use them as a part of your scheduled therapy sessions. Here are some pointers for including aromatherapy and herbalism in your witchcraft treatment practice:

Choose High-Quality Ingredients: For the best outcomes, pick high-quality herbs and essential oils. Look for ingredients that are organic and sustainably sourced.

Set Specific Intentions: Establish specific goals for your practice of aromatherapy and herbalism. This might entail concentrating on a particular problem you want to solve, like tension or anxiety. You can give the routine a distinct focus by setting clear intentions.

Prepare Your Remedies: Carefully prepare your herbal remedies and essential oils, using high-quality ingredients and cautious attention to directions. This will help to ensure the best results.

Use Your Remedies: Use your herbal remedies and essential oils as part of your regular self-care routine. This may involve drinking herbal tea before bed to promote relaxation, or using essential oils in a diffuser to create a calming atmosphere.

In conclusion, herbalism and aromatherapy are powerful techniques for promoting personal growth and healing in witchcraft therapy. By using the healing properties of plants and essential oils, you can support your physical, emotional, and spiritual well-being and promote a deeper sense of connection to the natural world. Additionally, these practices can help to reduce stress and promote a sense of calm. To incorporate herbalism and aromatherapy into your witchcraft therapy practice, it is important to choose high-quality ingredients, set clear intentions, and practice regularly. By doing so, you can enhance your experience and promote deeper healing and personal growth.

CHAPTER IV

Applying Witchcraft Therapy for Personal Growth

Overcoming negative patterns and behaviors

Applying witchcraft therapy for personal improvement requires overcoming destructive patterns and actions. We can be prevented from attaining our objectives and leading fulfilled lives by negative patterns and behaviors. We may recognize and get rid of these negative habits and behaviors using the witchcraft therapy concepts, leading to a life that is more positive and satisfying. In this section, we'll explore some of the essential procedures for applying witchcraft therapy to break negative habits and behaviors.

Identifying Negative Patterns and Behaviors

Identifying negative patterns and behaviors is the first step in getting rid of them. Self-sabotage, negative self-talk, and procrastination are just a few examples of negative patterns and behaviors. Keeping a journal and tracking your thoughts, feelings, and behaviors can be beneficial in identifying undesirable patterns and habits. By doing this, you can begin to recognize patterns and actions that might be preventing you from moving forward.

Using Witchcraft Therapy to Overcome Negative Patterns and Behaviors

Once you have identified negative patterns and behaviors, you can use witchcraft therapy to overcome them. Here are some key steps to follow:

Set an Intention

Set an intention to overcome your negative patterns and behaviors. This may involve concentrating on a particular problem you want to solve, such procrastination or unfavorable self-talk. You can give your practice direction and begin to move closer to your objectives by stating your intentions clearly.

Clear Your Energy

Utilize methods like ritualized energy cleaning, meditation, and visualization to clear your energy. You can eliminate bad feelings and thoughts and make room for more positive and clear personal growth by clearing your energy.

Use Positive Affirmations

Use positive affirmations to replace negative self-talk. You can change your thoughts and beliefs by repeating encouraging remarks to yourself, or affirmations. In order to replace negative self-talk and boost confidence, you may repeat the affirmation "I am capable and worthy of achieving my goals."

Create a New Narrative

Create a new narrative for yourself by focusing on positive outcomes and possibilities. You can begin to change your thoughts and beliefs by constructing a new story, which will help you lead a happier and more fulfilled life.

Practice Mindfulness

Maintaining presence of mind and awareness of one's internal experiences can be accomplished through the practice of mindfulness. Practicing mindfulness is bringing your attention to the here and now and allowing yourself to observe your thoughts and feelings without passing judgment on them. Through the practice of mindfulness, you can begin to see destructive patterns and behaviors as they occur and then take action to change them. This will allow you to make progress toward achieving your goals.

Use Rituals and Spells

Make use of rituals and spells to motivate your goals for personal development and support your ambitions. For instance, you could build a spell jar with herbs and crystals in order to boost your self-confidence and stop yourself from having negative thoughts about yourself.

Benefits of Overcoming Negative Patterns and Behaviors using Witchcraft Therapy

The use of witchcraft therapy to break free of destructive patterns and habits can have a lot of positive effects, including the following:

Increased Self-Awareness: By identifying negative patterns and behaviors, you can develop a deeper sense of self-awareness and understanding of your thoughts, emotions, and actions.
Increased Self-Confidence: It is possible to enhance one's self-confidence and belief in one's own capabilities through the utilization of positive affirmations and the creation of a new narrative for oneself.
Reduced levels of stress and anxiety: This can be achieved through the practice of mindfulness as well as energy clearing practices, which can also help to generate a sense of calm and overall well-being.
Increased Personal Development: If you use witchcraft therapy to overcome destructive patterns and routines, you can promote personal development and move closer to achieving your objectives.

Incorporating the Overcoming of Negative Patterns and Behaviors into Your Witchcraft Therapy Practice

It is crucial to have clear intentions, practice often, and be patient with yourself if you want to incorporate overcoming problematic patterns and behaviors into your witchcraft therapy practice. It takes time and effort to break harmful habits and behaviors, but if you are persistent and dedicated, you may achieve your goals and create a life that is more positive and satisfying. The following are some suggestions that can help you include this practice into your witchcraft therapy practice:

Start with Small Steps

Start with small steps to overcome negative patterns and behaviors. For instance, if procrastination is a problem for you, start by establishing a small objective and working toward it every day. You can get momentum and begin moving closer to your goals by starting small.

Use a Combination of Techniques

To overcome negative patterns and behaviors, combine several strategies. To support your intentions, you could, for instance, practice energy clearing techniques, mindfulness, and positive affirmations. Combining different methods will help you develop a more comprehensive and successful strategy for personal development.

Practice Regularly

To get momentum and move toward your goals, practice frequently. Setting aside time each day for rituals such as energy clearing rituals, meditation or visualization, are some of the techniques to achieve this. Regular practice will help you develop a durable and consistent strategy for personal development.

Be Patient with Yourself

Be patient with yourself and celebrate your progress along the way. Overcoming negative patterns and behaviors takes time and effort, and it is important to be kind and compassionate towards yourself as you work towards your goals.

Overall, applying witchcraft therapy for personal improvement requires overcoming destructive patterns and actions. We can have healthier and more fulfilled lives if we can recognize and get rid of our bad habits and behaviors. Setting clear aims, practicing often, and utilizing a variety of strategies are essential for employing witchcraft treatment to break bad habits and behaviors. You can accomplish your objectives and build a happier, more satisfying life by doing this. Remind yourself to appreciate your accomplishments, have patience with yourself, and remain dedicated to your goals.

Developing self-awareness and self-acceptance

One of the most important components of using witchcraft therapy for personal improvement is developing self-awareness and self-acceptance. We can have happier, more satisfying lives by coming to a deeper understanding of ourselves and accepting who we are. The fundamental steps to achieving self-awareness and self-acceptance through witchcraft therapy will be discussed in this section.

Understanding Self-Awareness

The capacity to detect and comprehend your thoughts, emotions, and behaviors is known as self-awareness. It involves being willing to accept responsibility for your actions as well as being honest with yourself about your strengths and flaws. Self-awareness is a crucial component of personal development because it enables you to identify the areas of your life where you wish to make adjustments and move forward with your plans.

Using Witchcraft Therapy to Develop Self-Awareness

Witchcraft therapy can be a powerful tool for developing self-awareness. Here are some key steps to follow:

Practice Mindfulness

Maintaining mindfulness will help you to be mindful of your thoughts, feelings, and actions. Focusing on the here and now while objectively evaluating your thoughts and feelings is what mindfulness implies. You can gain a deeper understanding of yourself and your thoughts and emotions by engaging in mindfulness practices.

Use Tarot and Divination

Use tarot and divination as tools for self-reflection and introspection. You can utilize tarot and divination to acquire understanding of your ideas, feelings, and actions as well as to assist you identify areas in which you desire to make changes.

Journaling

Journaling is another powerful tool for developing self-awareness. You can track your thoughts and feelings over time and get insight into patterns and behaviors that might be limiting you by maintaining a journal.

Seek Feedback

Seek feedback from trusted friends, family members, or a therapist. You may adjust your perspective on your ideas, feelings, and behaviors with the help of feedback, which can also help you identify areas where you wish to make changes.

Understanding Self-Acceptance

Self-acceptance is the capacity to accept oneself, qualities and flaws included. It involves accepting who you are as you are and treating yourself with kindness and respect. Self-acceptance is an essential part of personal growth, as it allows you to let go of negative self-talk and embrace a more positive and fulfilling life.

Using Witchcraft Therapy to Develop Self-Acceptance

Witchcraft therapy can be a powerful tool for developing self-acceptance. Here are some key steps to follow:

Use Positive Affirmations

Use positive affirmations to replace negative self-talk. You can change your thoughts and beliefs by repeating encouraging remarks to yourself, or affirmations. To combat negative self-talk and increase self-acceptance, you could, for instance, repeat the affirmation "I am worthy and deserving of love and respect."

Practice Gratitude

To keep your attention on the positive things of your life, cultivate gratitude. By expressing gratitude for what you have in your life, you can change your attention from negative self-talk to positive self-acceptance.

Use Rituals and Spells

Rituals and spells can help you achieve your goals and encourage self-acceptance. For instance, you may make a self-love spell jar with crystals and herbs to encourage self-acceptance and confidence.

Seek Support

Seek support from friends, family members, or a therapist. With the right kind of support, you may overcome any negative patterns or beliefs that might be preventing you from moving forward and improve your self-acceptance.

Benefits of Developing Self-Awareness and Self-Acceptance using Witchcraft Therapy

Benefits of practicing witchcraft therapy to increase one's self-awareness and self-acceptance include:
Enhanced Self-Esteem: You may increase your sense of self-worth and self-esteem by learning to embrace and understand who you are.

Reduced levels of stress and anxiety: This can be achieved through the cultivation of attitudes of mindfulness and appreciation, which in turn fosters a sense of inner peace and overall well-being.
Increased Personal Development: If you work on increasing your level of self-awareness and self-acceptance, you'll be able to identify the areas of your life in which you want to make adjustments and begin taking steps toward achieving your objectives.

More Positive Relationships: When you learn to accept yourself exactly as you are, you will be able to cultivate relationships with other people that are more positive and ultimately more satisfying.

Incorporating Self-Awareness and Self-Acceptance into Your Witchcraft Therapy Practice

To incorporate self-awareness and self-acceptance into your witchcraft therapy practice, it is important to set clear intentions, practice regularly, and be patient with yourself. The following are some tips that can help you include this practice into your witchcraft therapy practice:

Start with Small Steps

Start with small steps to develop self-awareness and self-acceptance. For example, you might start by practicing gratitude each day or using positive affirmations to replace negative self-talk.

Use a Combination of Techniques

Use a combination of techniques to develop self-awareness and self-acceptance. For example, you might use mindfulness, tarot and divination, and positive affirmations to support your intentions.

Practice Regularly

Maintaining a consistent practice can help you gain momentum and move closer to achieving your objectives. This may involve setting aside time each day for meditation, journaling, or self-reflection.

Be Patient with Yourself

Be patient with yourself and celebrate your progress along the way. Developing self-awareness and self-acceptance takes time and effort, and it is important to be kind and compassionate towards yourself as you work towards your goals.

In conclusion, using witchcraft therapy as a tool for personal development requires one to make significant progress in both becoming self-aware and accepting of oneself. It is possible to lead a life that is more uplifting and satisfying if we take the time to cultivate a better awareness of ourselves and accept who we are. It is necessary to make clear intentions, practice on a consistent basis, and use a combination of different approaches when engaging in witchcraft treatment in order to cultivate self-awareness and self-acceptance.

You will have a better chance of achieving your objectives and leading a life that is more positive and satisfying if you do so. Keep in mind that you should have patience with yourself, that you should celebrate your success, and that you should remain devoted to your goals.

Strengthening intuition and spiritual connection

A key component of using witchcraft therapy for personal development is strengthening intuition and spiritual connection. By developing a deeper understanding of our inner wisdom and spiritual connection, we can create a more fulfilling and meaningful life. In this article, we will explore some of the key steps to strengthening intuition and spiritual connection using witchcraft therapy.

Understanding Intuition and Spiritual Connection The ability to connect into our inner wisdom and make choices based on it called intuition. It involves having faith in oneself and one's instincts, as well as having the courage to take chances and change one's course in life. Building a connection with something more than ourselves, such as the universe, a higher power, or our own inner wisdom, is what it means to be spiritually connected.

Using Witchcraft Therapy to Strengthen Intuition and Spiritual Connection

Witchcraft therapy is a powerful instrument to strengthen spirituality and intuition. Here are some key steps to follow:

Practice Meditation and Visualization

To connect with your inner wisdom and improve your intuition, consider meditation and visualization. While visualization uses visuals to connect with your intuition and spiritual connection, meditation includes stilling the mind and concentrating on the here and now.

Use Tarot and Divination

Tarot and divination are useful tools for developing your spiritual connection and intuition. You can utilize tarot and divination to acquire understanding of your ideas, feelings, and actions as well as to assist you discover areas in which you desire to make changes.

Connect with Nature

Connect with nature to strengthen your spiritual connection. You can establish stronger spiritual connections and connect with the natural world by spending time in nature.

Practice Rituals and Spells

To deepen your spiritual connection and support your intentions, practice rituals and spells. For instance, you might establish a daily ritual for accessing your inner wisdom or employ spells to help you achieve your objectives.

Understanding the Benefits of Strengthening Intuition and Spiritual Connection

Intuition and spiritual connection can be strengthened for a variety of reasons, including:

Improved Decision Making: You may make more knowledgeable and assured decisions by strengthening your intuition.

Increased Creativity: If you are able to connect with your inner wisdom, you will be able to unleash your creativity and open up new avenues of thought and viewpoints.

Greater Sense of Purpose: By strengthening your spiritual connection, you can develop a greater sense of purpose and meaning in your life.

More Positive connections: You will be able to cultivate more positive and rewarding connections with individuals if you connect with your intuition and your spiritual connection.

Incorporating Intuition and Spiritual Connection into Your Witchcraft Therapy Practice

It is essential to have crystal clear intentions, engage in consistent practice, and exercise patience with oneself if you wish to successfully include intuition and spiritual connection into your witchcraft therapy practice. The following are some tips that can help you include this practice into your witchcraft therapy practice:

Start with Small Steps

Begin by taking small actions to improve your intuitive abilities and connection to the spiritual world. For instance, you could begin by learning how to meditate or by reading tarot cards in order to gain insight into the thoughts and feelings that you are currently experiencing.

Use a Combination of Techniques

To improve your spiritual connection and intuition, combine various strategies. To support your desires, you could, for instance, practice meditation, tarot card readings, divination, rituals, and spells.

Practice Regularly

Regular practice will help you gain momentum and progress toward your objectives. This may involve setting aside time each day for meditation, journaling, or connecting with nature.

Be Patient with Yourself

Be patient with yourself and celebrate your progress along the way. Strengthening intuition and spiritual connection takes time and effort, and it is important to be kind and compassionate towards yourself as you work towards your goals.

In conclusion, strengthening intuition and spiritual connection is an essential part of applying witchcraft therapy for personal growth. By developing a deeper understanding of our inner wisdom and spiritual connection, we can create a more fulfilling and meaningful life. To strengthen intuition and spiritual connection using witchcraft therapy, it is important to set clear intentions, practice regularly, and use a combination of techniques. By doing so, you can achieve your goals and create a more positive and fulfilling life. Remind yourself to appreciate your accomplishments, have patience with yourself, and remain dedicated to your goals.

You can strengthen your spiritual connection, increase self-awareness and self-acceptance, and connect with your intuition by adding the witchcraft therapy techniques into your personal growth journey. These strategies help you break bad habits and behaviors, experience emotional and physical healing, and build a happier, more satisfying life.

Keep in mind that the path to personal growth is not always simple, and it is essential to ask for help and advice when you need it. With the use of witchcraft therapy, you can navigate your personal growth journey with the support of additional assistance and direction from a therapist or spiritual mentor.

As a result, witchcraft therapy is a potent instrument for personal development that can assist you in strengthening your spiritual connection, developing self-awareness and self-acceptance, and connecting with your inner wisdom. You can overcome unfavorable patterns and behaviors, experience emotional and physical healing, and build a more positive and satisfying existence by implementing witchcraft therapy techniques into your daily life.

Creating a sense of empowerment and self-worth

An important component of using witchcraft therapy for personal improvement is developing a sense of empowerment and self-worth. We may accomplish our objectives and have more satisfied lives by strengthening our sense of self-worth and personal power. In this section, we'll look at some of the essential procedures for applying witchcraft therapy to foster a sense of empowerment and self-worth.

Understanding Empowerment and Self-Worth

Taking charge of your life and making choices that are consistent with your values and objectives is the process of becoming empowered. It involves acquiring a sense of personal power and authority, being willing to take risks and make changes in your life. For you to achieve your objectives and lead a satisfying life, you must believe in your own value and worthiness.

Using Witchcraft Therapy to Create a Sense of Empowerment and Self-Worth

Witchcraft therapy has the potential to be a potent tool for fostering self-worth and empowerment. Here are some key steps to follow:

Practice Self-Love and Self-Care

To increase your sense of value, work on your self-love and self-care. This could entail setting aside time each day to engage in self-care rituals like bathing or meditation or using encouraging affirmations to boost self-esteem.

Use Spells and Rituals

To strengthen yourself and support your intentions, use spells and rituals. For instance, you might cast a spell to make a desire come true or design a ceremony to acknowledge your accomplishments.

Connect with Community

Make connections with like-minded people to gain a sense of empowerment and support. This can entail signing up for a coven or going to workshops and activities centered around witchcraft therapy.

Develop a Strong Personal Practice

Create a solid personal routine that supports your objectives and fosters your sense of self-determination and agency. This may involve creating a daily practice for connecting with your intuition, practicing meditation or visualization, or using tarot and divination to gain insights into your thoughts and emotions.

Understanding the Benefits of Empowerment and Self-Worth

There are several advantages to developing a sense of empowerment and self-worth, including:
Increased Self-Confidence: If you work on improving your feeling of self-worth, you'll find that you have increased self-confidence in both your abilities and your worthiness.

Increased Resilience: It is possible to increase your resilience and become better equipped to deal with difficulties and obstacles if you give yourself more authority and take charge of your life.
More Positive Relationships: When you learn to appreciate who you are and what you bring to the world, you can cultivate relationships with other people that are more positive and ultimately more satisfying.
Greater Success: You will have more success if you cultivate a sense of personal power and agency. This will allow you to accomplish your ambitions and lead a life that is more satisfying.

Incorporating Empowerment and Self-Worth into Your Witchcraft Therapy Practice

To incorporate empowerment and self-worth into your witchcraft therapy practice, it is important to set clear intentions, practice regularly, and be patient with yourself. The following are some tips that can help you include this practice into your witchcraft therapy practice:

Start with Small Steps

To construct a feeling of self-worth and empowerment, it is best to begin with small steps. You may, for instance, begin by engaging in rituals of self-care or by employing positive affirmations in order to strengthen your sense of self-worth.

Use a Combination of Techniques

Make use of a variety of strategies to cultivate a feeling of self-worth and empowerment in yourself. To help you in achieving your objectives, you might, for instance, employ spells and rituals, make connections with members of a community, and cultivate a personal practice.

Practice Regularly

Maintaining a consistent practice can help you gain momentum and move closer to achieving your objectives. To do this, you might need to schedule time in your timetable every day for things like meditation, self-care, or practicing your craft.

Be Patient with Yourself

Be patient with yourself and celebrate your progress along the way. It takes time and effort to build a sense of empowerment and self-worth, and it is essential to be kind and compassionate towards yourself while you work towards achieving your goals in order to ensure that you are able to do so.

Overall, when used for the purpose of personal development, witchcraft therapy must always begin with the cultivation of a sense of empowerment and worthiness within oneself. We may achieve our ambitions and lead a life that is more satisfying if we have a deeper awareness of our own value and our capacity for personal power. It is necessary to practice self-love and self-care, utilize spells and rituals, connect with community, and cultivate an effective personal practice in order to generate a sense of empowerment and self-worth through the usage of witchcraft therapy. Don't forget to be patient with yourself, acknowledge your accomplishments, and remain devoted to the goals you've set for yourself.

You can strengthen your spiritual connection, connect with your intuition, gain self-awareness and self-acceptance, and develop a sense of empowerment and self-worth by combining the witchcraft therapy techniques into your personal growth journey. These strategies help you overcome bad habits and behaviors, experience emotional and physical healing, and build a healthier, more satisfying life.

Keep in mind that the path to personal growth is not always simple, and it is crucial to ask for help and advice when you need it. With the use of witchcraft therapy, you can navigate your personal growth journey with the aid of additional support and guidance from a therapist or spiritual advisor.

In conclusion, witchcraft therapy is a potent instrument for personal growth that can assist you in establishing a greater spiritual connection, connecting with your inner wisdom, growing in self-awareness and self-acceptance, and developing a sense of empowerment and self-worth. You can get rid of bad habits and behaviors, experience emotional and physical healing, and build a happier, more satisfying existence by implementing witchcraft therapy techniques into your daily life.

CHAPTER V

Incorporating Witchcraft Therapy into Your Daily Life

Developing a daily witchcraft practice

Witchcraft therapy can be a very powerful tool for personal and spiritual growth if you incorporate it into your daily life. Developing a daily witchcraft practice involves setting intentions, establishing rituals, and building a connection to your intuition and spiritual guidance. We shall examine some essential steps for creating a daily witchcraft practice in this section.

Step 1: Set Intentions

Setting specific intention for your practice is the first step in creating a daily witchcraft routine. This include deciding how you want to use witchcraft treatment to promote your personal growth and spiritual development, as well as identifying your goals and values.. Some examples of intentions might include:
- Developing a stronger connection to your intuition and spiritual guidance
- Overcoming negative patterns and behaviors

- Cultivating self-love and self-acceptance

- Manifesting abundance and prosperity

- Healing emotionally and physically

You can develop a structure for your everyday witchcraft practice and keep your attention on your objectives if you make your intentions crystal clear beforehand.

Step 2: Establish Rituals

After you have decided what you want to accomplish with your practice, the next stage is to create rituals that will help you accomplish those goals. This might involve creating a sacred space for your practice, choosing specific tools or objects to use in your practice, and developing a daily routine for your practice. Some examples of rituals might include:

- Lighting candles or incense to create a calming and meditative atmosphere
- Using crystals or other objects to connect with your intuition and spiritual guidance

- Practicing visualization or meditation to focus your intentions and connect with your inner wisdom

- Incorporating tarot or divination to gain insights into your thoughts and emotions

- Using herbs, oils, or other natural remedies to support physical and emotional healing

By establishing rituals that support your intentions, you can create a consistent and meaningful daily practice.

Step 3: Connect with Your Intuition and Spiritual Guidance

The final step in developing a daily witchcraft practice is to connect with your intuition and spiritual guidance. This involves developing a deeper understanding of your own inner wisdom and connecting with the divine or universal energy that surrounds us all. Some ways to connect with your intuition and spiritual guidance might include:

- Practicing mindfulness and staying present in the moment

- Using meditation or visualization to quiet the mind and connect with your inner wisdom

- Using any form of divination, such as tarot cards to obtain insight into your feelings and ideas

- Interacting with the natural world and its vitality through spending time in nature

- Using mantras or affirmations to direct your objectives and establish a connection with the divine

You can gain a greater understanding of yourself and your place in the world by connecting with your intuition and spiritual guidance.

Step 4: Build a Community

Creating a group of like-minded people can offer support and direction as you establish your daily witchcraft practice. This could entail signing up for a coven or going to workshops and activities centered around witchcraft therapy. You can gain a sense of community and support by making connections with people who have similar interests and aims to your own.

Step 5: Practice Consistency

When it comes to creating a daily witchcraft practice, consistency is essential.. It is important to make time for your practice each day, even if it is just a few minutes. This can help you to build momentum and stay focused on your goals.

Step 6: Be Open to Growth and Change

As you develop your daily witchcraft practice, it is important to remain open to growth and change. This might involve trying new rituals or techniques, or revisiting your intentions and goals. By staying open to new experiences and perspectives, you can continue to evolve and grow as a person.

Tips for Developing a Daily Witchcraft Practice

- Set aside time each day for your practice, even if it is just a few minutes.
- Start with small steps and build momentum over time.

- Experiment with different techniques and rituals to find what works best for you.

- Be patient with yourself and celebrate your progress along the way.

- Seek support and guidance when needed, from a therapist or spiritual advisor.

Benefits of a Daily Witchcraft Practice

Developing a daily witchcraft practice can provide a number of benefits, including:

- A deeper sense of self-awareness and self-acceptance

- A stronger connection to your intuition and spiritual guidance

- Increased resilience and coping skills

- Improved emotional and physical health

- Greater personal power and agency

Witchcraft therapy can be a very effective tool for spiritual and personal development if you incorporate it into your daily life. You can develop a meaningful and rewarding daily practice that fosters your spiritual and personal development by setting intentions, establishing rituals, connecting with your intuition and spiritual guidance, creating a community, engaging in consistency, and remaining open to growth and change.

Maintaining a connection to nature and the seasons

You can strengthen your connections to the natural world and develop a stronger sense of purpose and meaning in life by including a connection to nature and the seasons into your regular witchcraft therapy practice. You can keep a strong connection to the natural world and enjoy all of its advantages by tuning into the rhythms of the natural world, practicing mindfulness in nature, celebrating the seasons, incorporating nature into your practice, and using eco-friendly practices.

Step 1: Tune into the Rhythms of the Natural World

Maintaining a connection to nature and the seasons requires tuning into the rhythms of the natural world. This may entail keeping an eye out for the fall's leaf color changes, paying attention to the moon's phases, or keeping track on the stars' motions. We can gain a greater understanding of the complexity and beauty of the natural world by learning to tune into these rhythms.

Spending time in nature on a daily basis, even if it's only for a short period of time, is one method to get in rhythm with the cycles that govern the natural world. This has the potential to help us feel more connected to the natural world around us, as well as providing a sense of grounding and tranquility.

Step 2: Practice Mindfulness in Nature

Maintaining a connection to the natural world also requires engaging in important activities like practicing mindfulness in natural settings. This could mean participating in activities such as going on hikes in the great outdoors, engaging in activities such as yoga or meditation outside, or simply spending time in quiet reflection and consideration. Through the practice of mindfulness in natural settings, we can develop a sense of present and awareness, both of which can assist us in experiencing a greater sense of connection to the world around us.

Take a walk in the woods and concentrate on experiencing the environment with all of your senses as you practice mindfulness there. Spend some time observing the hues, textures, and aromas found in nature. Take in the sounds of the animals and birds. By doing this, we can strengthen our connections to nature and feel more present in the moment.

Step 3: Celebrate the Seasons

Maintaining a connection to nature and the changing of the seasons requires a number of different activities, one of which is celebrating the changing of the seasons. This might involve observing the solstices and equinoxes, celebrating holidays and festivals that are rooted in nature, or simply taking time to appreciate the changing colors and rhythms of the natural world. We can connect with life's cycles and feel more at one with the environment around us by celebrating the seasons.

Making a nature altar or shrine for your home or outdoor space is one way to commemorate the changing of the seasons. The natural environment and the varying seasons might be honored here. To decorate the altar and foster a sense of regard for the natural world, you can use organic items like flowers, leaves, and stones.

Step 4: Incorporate Nature into Your Practice

You can strengthen your connection to the natural world by including nature in your witchcraft therapy practices.

This might involve using natural materials like herbs and crystals in your spells and rituals, or creating an outdoor altar or shrine to honor the natural world. You can develop a deeper sense of reverence and connection to nature by incorporating it into your practice.

Utilizing organic components in your spells and rituals, like as herbs and crystals, is one method to include nature into your practice. To understand the natural world and its energy, you can also use divination techniques like tarot.

Step 5: Engage in Eco-Friendly Practices

Another method to keep a connection to nature and the seasons is to conduct eco-friendly behaviors. We may contribute to preserving and protecting the natural world, to which we are so intimately related, by minimizing our impact on the environment.

Reducing our usage of plastic, using less energy and water, supporting regional and sustainable businesses, recycling, and composting are a few examples of eco-friendly behaviors.

In conclusion, maintaining a connection to nature and the seasons can be a powerful tool for personal growth and spiritual development. By tuning into the rhythms of the natural world, practicing mindfulness in nature, celebrating the seasons, incorporating nature into your practice, and engaging in eco-friendly practices, you can deepen your connection to the natural world and experience the many benefits that come with it.

Some additional tips for maintaining a connection to nature and the seasons include:

- Study the mythology and folklore of different cultures related to nature and the seasons

- Volunteer for environmental organizations or participate in local clean-up efforts
- Learn about local flora and fauna and their medicinal or spiritual properties
- Create a garden or indoor plantscape to bring the energy of nature into your home
- Practice gratitude for the natural world and the gifts it provides

Benefits of Maintaining a Connection to Nature and the Seasons

Maintaining a connection to nature and the seasons can provide a number of benefits, including:
- A deeper sense of connection and reverence for the natural world
- Increased feelings of calm and peace

- Improved physical and emotional health

- A greater sense of purpose and meaning in life

- A stronger connection to the divine

You can strengthen your connection to the natural world and develop a stronger sense of purpose and meaning in life by incorporating a connection to nature and the seasons into your daily witchcraft treatment practice. You can keep a strong connection to the natural world and enjoy all of its advantages by tuning into the rhythms of the natural world, practicing mindfulness in nature, enjoying the seasons, incorporating nature into your practice, and using eco-friendly practices.

Finding a community of like-minded individuals

Finding a group of people who share your beliefs might be crucial when integrating witchcraft treatment into your daily life. Being a part of a group of people who share your beliefs can provide you a sense of community and support, as well as possibilities for learning and development. In this article, we will explore some key steps to finding a community of like-minded individuals to support your witchcraft therapy practice.

Step 1: Identify Your Interests and Goals

Identifying your interests and objectives is the first step in finding a group of people who share them. This could entail looking into various aspects of witchcraft therapy, such as meditation, divination, or herbalism, and determining which sections attract your interest the most.

It is also a good idea to give some thought to the objectives you wish to accomplish with your witchcraft therapy practice. Do you wish to strengthen your connection to the spiritual world, work through your emotional problems, or enhance your intuitive abilities? If you are aware of your objectives, you will be better able to locate groups of people and communities that have interests that are congruent with your own and that can offer assistance in accomplishing your objectives.

Step 2: Attend Local Events and Gatherings

Going to gatherings and events that are held locally is a fantastic way to meet people in your neighborhood who share your interests and values. This might involve attending a local coven meeting, attending a pagan festival or gathering, or participating in a group meditation or ritual.

By participating in these activities, you will have the opportunity to connect with new people who share your interests and ambitions, and you will also start to establish a sense of community and support for yourself.

Step 3: Join Online Communities and Forums

Participating in local events is one of the best ways to interact with others who share similar interests; but, joining online communities and forums may also be very beneficial. You can interact with other people, ask questions of them, and share your own experiences by participating in one of the many online communities or forums that are devoted to witchcraft therapy and other related issues.

Some of the most well-known communities and forums that can be found online are Witch Vox, the Witchcraft community on Reddit, and many Facebook groups that are centered on witchcraft therapy.

Step 4: Seek Out a Mentor or Teacher

Finding a teacher or mentor to guide you through the process of practicing witchcraft therapy can be another beneficial method to interact with people who share your values and expand your knowledge of the subject matter. A mentor or teacher can provide guidance and support as you explore your practice, and can also help you to connect with other individuals in the community.

You may want to look into finding a local teacher or mentor through events and meetings in your area. Alternatively, you might look into finding online resources and courses to connect with experienced practitioners.

Step 5: Start Your Own Group or Circle

If you live in an area that lacks a community of people who share your values and perspectives, you might want to think about establishing your own support group or social circle. This can be an excellent method to interact with other people who share your interests and objectives, and it also has the potential to create chances for learning and development.

If you want to form your own group or circle, you should think about reaching out to other people in your neighborhood who share your interests and objectives, and you should organize regular meetings or gatherings to learn about the many parts of witchcraft therapy.

Tips for Finding a Community of Like-Minded Individuals

- Identify your interests and goals for your witchcraft therapy practice
- Attend local events and gatherings

- Join online communities and forums

- Seek out a mentor or teacher

- Consider starting your own group or circle

Benefits of Finding a Community of Like-Minded Individuals

Discovering a group of people that share your values and perspectives can result in numerous advantages, including the following:

- A sense of belonging and support

- Opportunities for learning and growth

- Access to new resources and information

- Inspiration and motivation to deepen your practice

- A space for you to talk about your experiences and make more meaningful connections with other people.

Overall, when adopting witchcraft treatment into your everyday life, one of the most critical steps is to locate a group of people that share your values and perspectives. You can connect with others who share your interests and goals, deepen your knowledge and understanding of witchcraft therapy, and cultivate a sense of community and support by participating in local events and gatherings, becoming a member of online communities and forums, seeking out a mentor or teacher, or starting your own group or circle. By connecting with like-minded individuals, you can enhance your personal growth and spiritual development, and find inspiration and motivation to continue exploring and expanding your practice.

Whether you are just beginning your practice of witchcraft therapy or have been pursuing this path for some time, finding a community of like-minded individuals can help you feel supported and connected as you navigate the ups and downs of your journey. You are able to continue to expand and deepen your practice if you have the correct community and support behind you. At the same time, you are able to share your knowledge and experiences with others in the community.

When looking for a community of people who share your beliefs, it is vital to keep in mind that everyone's path is different, and there is no "right" way to to engage in witchcraft therapy. This is something you should keep in mind as you search for such a community. As you explore your practice, while you should be open to gaining knowledge from others, you should also trust your own intuition and the wisdom that resides within you.

In addition, it can be helpful to approach these communities and gatherings with an open mind and heart, and to be respectful and supportive of others in the community. You may help to create a strong and dynamic community that encourages the personal growth and spiritual development of all of its members by fostering a sense of mutual respect and support among the members of the community you are a part of.

In conclusion, one of the most important aspects of implementing witchcraft therapy into one's everyday life is to look for a community of people who share similar values and perspectives. Connecting with others who share your interests and objectives can provide a sense of belonging and support, as well as opportunities for learning and development. You can achieve this by participating in local events and gatherings, becoming a member of online communities and forums, looking for a mentor or teacher, or beginning your own group or circle. You can further your practice, improve your personal growth, and advance your spiritual development by embracing the power of community, which also affords you the opportunity to share your insights and experiences with others who are on a similar journey.

Integrating witchcraft into your spiritual practice

Integrating witchcraft into your spiritual practice can be a powerful way to deepen your connection to the divine and enhance your personal growth and spiritual development. Whether you are new to witchcraft therapy or have been practicing for some time, incorporating witchcraft into your spiritual practice can provide a wide range of benefits. Some of these benefits include increased intuition and a deeper spiritual connection, enhanced creativity and inspiration, and a greater sense of purpose and meaning in life.

In this section, we will discuss some of the most important stages that need to be taken in order to successfully include witchcraft into your spiritual practice. These steps involve exploring your spiritual beliefs, incorporating witchcraft into your daily routine, and cultivating a sense of connection with and reverence for the divine.

Step 1: Explore Your Spiritual Beliefs

The first thing you need to do to incorporate witchcraft into your spiritual practice is to explore the values and beliefs that guide your spiritual path. This might involve exploring different spiritual traditions, studying the mythology and folklore associated with witchcraft, or engaging in meditation or prayer to connect with the divine.

You can start to acquire a stronger sense of connection and reverence for the divine as well as start to understand how witchcraft treatment can improve your current spiritual practice by exploring your spiritual beliefs and values.

Step 2: Incorporate Witchcraft into Your Daily Routine
Another critical step toward integrating witchcraft into your spiritual practice is to incorporate it into your daily routine. This may entail introducing daily rituals or practices into your schedule, such as tarot reading, visualization, or meditation.

You may give your life structure and meaning by adopting these practices into your daily routine. You can also strengthen your relationship with the divine and your inner wisdom.

Step 3: Cultivate a Sense of Connection and Respect for the Divine
Integrating witchcraft into your spiritual practice requires you to develop a sense of connection to and reverence for the divine. This might involve spending time in nature, engaging in rituals or ceremonies, or engaging in spiritual practices that connect you with the divine.

You can strengthen your spiritual connection, improve your personal growth and spiritual development, and find more fulfillment in life by developing a sense of connection and reverence for the divine.

Tips for Integrating Witchcraft into Your Spiritual Practice

- Explore your spiritual beliefs and values

- Incorporate witchcraft into your daily routine

- Cultivate a sense of connection and reverence for the divine
- Try out various techniques and rituals to see what works best for you.
- Be open to learning and growing in your practice

Benefits of Integrating Witchcraft into Your Spiritual Practice

Witchcraft can be included into your spiritual practice for a variety of reasons, such as:
- Increased intuition and spiritual connection

- Enhanced creativity and inspiration

- Greater sense of purpose and meaning in life

- Improved physical and emotional health

- Deeper connection to the divine

In conclusion, integrating witchcraft into your spiritual practice can be a powerful way to deepen your connection to the divine and enhance your personal growth and spiritual development. You can strengthen your spiritual connection and find more meaning in life by exploring your spiritual ideas and values, incorporating witchcraft into your everyday routine, and building a sense of connection and reverence for the divine. Integrating witchcraft into your spiritual practice can offer a wide range of advantages and chances for growth and transformation, whether you are new to witchcraft treatment or have been practicing for some time.

CONCLUSION

Summary of witchcraft's therapeutic benefits

Witchcraft therapy is a powerful instrument for healing and personal development. An individual can access their inner wisdom, establish a connection with the divine, and resolve their emotional and physical problems by using techniques including meditation, visualization, spellwork, and divination. In this article, we will recap the benefits of using witchcraft as a therapeutic tool, including enhanced self-awareness, emotional healing, physical
healing, and spiritual growth.

1. Enhanced Self-Awareness

One of the primary benefits of using witchcraft as a therapeutic tool is enhanced self-awareness. By engaging in practices such as meditation and visualization, individuals can tap into their inner wisdom and gain a deeper understanding of their thoughts, feelings, and behaviors. This increased self-awareness can help individuals to identify negative patterns and behaviors and work towards positive change and personal growth.

2. Emotional Healing

Witchcraft therapy can also be a powerful tool for emotional healing. By working through emotional issues such as trauma, anxiety, and depression, individuals can release negative emotions and gain a greater sense of peace and calm. Practices such as spellwork and ritual can also provide a sense of empowerment and control, helping individuals to feel more confident and capable in their daily lives.

3. Physical Healing

In addition to emotional healing, witchcraft therapy can also be beneficial for physical healing. Practices such as herbalism and aromatherapy can be used to support physical healing and wellness, while practices such as energy work can help to release physical tension and pain. Individuals can promote their physical health and well-being by utilizing the body's own healing capabilities and interacting with the earth's energies.

4. Spiritual Growth

Witchcraft therapy is a potent instrument for spiritual development, too. Individuals can strengthen their spiritual connection and find more meaning and purpose in life by interacting with the energy of the earth and the elements and connecting with the divine. Tarot reading and other divination techniques can also offer guidance and insight into life's difficulties, assisting people in following their path more deliberately and with better clarity.

5. Incorporating Witchcraft Therapy into Your Daily Life

It's crucial to incorporate these techniques into your daily life if you want to gain from witchcraft therapy. This might involve developing a daily meditation practice, creating a sacred space for ritual and spellwork, or working with herbs and essential oils to support your physical and emotional health. By incorporating these practices into your daily routine, you can deepen your connection to the divine, support your personal growth and healing, and gain a greater sense of purpose and meaning in life.

In summary, using witchcraft as a therapeutic tool can provide a wealth of benefits for personal growth and healing. From enhanced self-awareness to emotional and physical healing to spiritual growth, witchcraft therapy can help individuals to tap into their inner wisdom, connect with the divine, and work through life's challenges with greater clarity and intention. By incorporating these practices into your daily life, you can support your personal growth and healing and gain a greater sense of purpose and meaning in life.

Final ideas and encouragement to use witchcraft for self-improvement

As we come to the end of this book, we hope that you have gained a deeper understanding of witchcraft therapy and its potential for personal growth and healing. We encourage you to continue on your journey, exploring new rituals and methods, and making contact with the divine in your own special way, whether you are new to witchcraft or have been pursuing this path for some time.

1. There isn't a one "right" approach to perform witchcraft therapy, however there are a few guiding concepts that can help you on your journey:

2. Trust your intuition: Witchcraft therapy is based on a strong belief in your own inner wisdom and intuition. You can find clarity and direction as you face the obstacles of life by connecting with this inner voice.
3. Embrace the power of intention: A key component of witchcraft therapy is setting specific intentions. By focusing your energy and attention on what you want to manifest in your life, you can work towards positive change and personal growth.

4. Connect with the natural wrotld: Witchcraft therapy is founded on a strong connection to nature. You can strengthen your spiritual connection and find more meaning in life by spending time in nature, working with herbs and other natural materials, and observing the seasonal cycles.
5. Cultivate a sense of community: Finally, an important component of witchcraft therapy is creating a sense of community and support. Finding like-minded people to share your path with can offer a sense of belonging and support, as well as chances for learning and growth, whether you connect with other practitioners in person or online.

We advise you to approach your practice as you proceed along your path with curiosity, openness, and a desire to learn and grow. By embracing the power of witchcraft therapy, you can enhance your personal growth and healing, deepen your connection to the divine, and gain a greater sense of purpose and meaning in life.

We hope that this book has given you a thorough understanding of witchcraft therapy and its potential for healing and personal development. You can strengthen your connection to the divine, aid in your personal growth and healing, and find more meaning and purpose in life by incorporating techniques like meditation, visualization, spellwork, and divination into your daily life. Whether you are just beginning your journey or have been on this path for some time, we encourage you to keep moving forward by following your instincts, believing in the power of intention, interacting with nature, and developing a sense of support and community.

Thank you for buying and reading/ listening to our book. If you found this book useful/ helpful please take a few minutes and leave a review on the platform where you purchased our book. Your feedback matters greatly to us.

www.ingramcontent.com/pod-product-compliance
Lightning Source LLC
LaVergne TN
LVHW021828060526
838201LV00058B/3562